Wrapped in His Arms of Love

Printed in the United States of America.

ISBN: 978-1-59571-833-4
Library of Congress Control Number: 2012918252

Designed and published by

Word Association Publishers
205 Fifth Avenue
Tarentum, Pennsylvania 15084

www.wordassociation.com
1.800.827.7903

Wrapped in His Arms of Love

KIMBERLY McCORMICK

WORD ASSOCIATION PUBLISHERS
www.wordassociation.com
1.800.827.7903

For Rod

You are in every way the definition of Christian love.
You were with me every step of this journey.

Love is patient, love is kind. It does not envy, it does not boast, it is not proud. It is not rude, it is not self-seeking, it is not easily angered, it keeps no record of wrongs. Love does not delight in evil but rejoices with the truth. It always protects, always trusts, always hopes, always perseveres.

Love never fails...

I Corinthians 13:4-8(NIV)

Contents

Preface

This is a diary of my eighteen month journey from a life of good health to one dealing with the reality of a life-threatening illness.

I believe we can choose the path we walk even in the face of sobering and threatening circumstances. Had I focused entirely on everything that was sad and awful about my illness, I would have missed all the great things in life that were still going on around me. That is not to say that I didn't have bad days or days when my spirit was deflated. My family was anxious about my illness; they felt vulnerable too. I tried not to burden them further with my tears and anxiety—sometimes that meant crying alone in the shower, but I never *felt* alone. Their love and support was unending. I gained strength and resilience by choosing to focus on the love, both earthly and heavenly, embracing me on all sides.

Every individual chooses his or her own way to deal with life's adversities, no way is right or wrong. I simply chose a path that allowed me to realize my life was still blessed, even in the midst of my storm.

It is my hope that sharing my story may help others whose lives take them on a similar path.

Acknowledgements

Andrea Tice served as my guiding spirit when she raised thought-provoking questions after reading my first drafts. Her guidance brought out emotions I had not considered. Not only is Andrea a wonderful editor, she is a wonderful person, too. Thank you, Andrea, for your willingness to follow God's lead when I made that first call asking for your help. I believe God has great things in store for your gifted writing abilities and editing advice. Continue to follow His lead.

Cynthia Nelson was the next editor to take me under her wing. I chose Cindy to edit my story because she believes editing needs to be respectful and true to the author's own voice. She understood I wanted each reader to feel as if he or she was a friend with whom I was sharing my story. Thank you, Cindy, for being sensitive to my desires and my ultimate goal of creating a book that may touch the lives of everyday people. You certainly helped to shape my story into one that may influence and affect many.

Thomas Shumaker, my stepfather, has supported my efforts from the first time I mentioned using my writing/speaking abilities as an avenue for fund raising. He offered suggestions for my text, as well as ideas for organizing the manuscript. By finding Word Association Publishers for me, he saved me countless hours of legwork. I will always appreciate you, Tom, and the way you encourage me to reach my full potential in life.

Finally, my husband, Rod, who is and always has been my number one supporter. No matter what adventure I wish to embark on, he is behind me, unselfishly allowing me to explore so many areas of interest. Thank you, Rod, for helping me turn a dark night into a bright sunrise.

My gratitude and appreciation to all those who have sustained and nurtured me throughout this period cannot adequately be expressed. Clearly, I could not have endured these months without the love and support of my husband, family, co-workers, medical providers, friends, and most especially, my faith in the love of God and utmost confidence that His plans for me include many more steps to travel before I am home with Him.

1

Diagnosis

In only a few seconds our lives can be changed forever. Perhaps changed for the good, a new baby is born or your love proposes marriage. Or maybe like me, those few seconds turn a pleasant, somewhat predictable middle-class life into a life filled with unknowns. A time when tears are shed, yet laughter and love follow. A time when emotions are so raw and real you are certain you have never felt these emotions in your life before. I experienced those life-changing seconds on March 1, 2011. The events of the day play over and over again, like a movie in my mind.

Racing about my classroom in preparation for the evening's activities, I attempt to straighten up. My desk shows the remains of the day's work. Books need to be shelved, papers need to be filed and somewhere under this mess are the supplies I need for the night. Sharpened pencils and erasers are lined up on my horseshoe-shaped desk, waiting to be used by our guests. Just a few minutes more is all I need to be ready for our evening program.

I work as a Reading Specialist/Music Teacher for the Wilmington Area School District. On this particular evening the reading and math teachers have a Family Math Night scheduled in conjunction with Westminster College and their education students. We are expecting a great turnout of parents and students. The excitement is already brewing as we change from our school dress clothes into tennis shoes and jeans. Being more comfortable is one thing we teachers appreciate about the night.

A quick scan of my classroom assures me that it is now ready for action. Even the chalkboard is gleaming black thanks to our devoted custodial staff. Before the rush of registration begins, I decide to check my phone for any texts or messages. Digging through my sack purse to find my phone presents a challenge. I pull out my wallet, my makeup satchel, my keys, my hand sanitizer…where is that phone…this always happens when I'm in a hurry.

Finally, success! Flipping open the phone, there is one message waiting for me. It's from my doctor's office. My breath catches, and I am immediately alert. With a slightly shaking hand, I key in my password and press one for new messages, "Kim, this is Dr. Rifaat Bassaly's office calling. He would like you to stop down today to see him after school. Please give us a call back."

A flash of what's to come hits me. They are about to deliver some life-changing news. After all, I am now on my tenth different gynecological test to solve the mystery of my bad Pap test result the previous August.

My thoughts go back to the day of the first test results…

August, 2010.

It's a typical summer day, and I'm busy running around town on errands. A nurse from Dr. Bassaly's office calls my cell to tell me that my Pap test results are in. The doctor wants to see me to discuss these results. I learn that AGUS or "atypical glandular cells of undetermined significance," are present. Red flag! At least to Dr. Bassaly it is. It doesn't really bother me. I feel great, I eat healthfully and exercise. I don't drink or smoke. Heck, I do everything right when it comes to my health. It never occurs to me that anything could be wrong.

Dr. Bassaly is concerned, though. He follows up the initial test with a colposcopy, (biopsy of the cervix) and an endometrial biopsy of the uterus, as well as an intravaginal sonogram of the ovaries. He also has me get a CA 125 blood test done, which helps detect cancer. CA 125 is a protein that is typically higher in concentration when tumor cells are present. Guess what? All is well. There is a small cyst on one ovary, but the doctor believes it will most likely be gone after my next menstrual cycle. I'm happy, but not surprised, to hear this news. It's not uncommon for a woman to have an ovarian cyst. Normally, they go away on their own, and because I'm feeling fine, this doesn't worry me.

Dr. Bassaly is still concerned, though, and tells me he wants to recheck everything in three months. This plan is fine with me. For the next three months, life goes on as usual.

Early November, 2010

It is three months later. Dr. Bassaly orders the CA 125 blood test again. He performs a second Pap test and intravaginal sonogram. Once again, all test results are fine. Dr. Bassaly asks me to return in three more months. I agree and applaud him for being cautious and thorough. On my way out, I notice The Physicians Prayer framed on Dr. Bassaly's desk. Reading this gives me reassurance. *Lord, please guide me as I treat my patients. Help me to be wise and compassionate. Allow me to see their problems through your eyes. May I always be humble for you are the Great Physician. Amen*

With Dr. Bassaly following these prayerful words, I am in good hands.

Late November, 2010

Thanksgiving break is nearly upon us. All day at school I feel a throbbing pain in my lower back/upper left hip area. By the end of the day, it is difficult for me to walk. As soon as I arrive home, I rest uncomfortably on the couch until Rod is finished working. By this time, I know I need help.

"Rod, I need to go the emergency room. There is definitely something wrong with me." Because of my recent appointments and tests with Dr. Bassaly, I'm quite concerned. At the emergency room, the ER doctor decides to call Dr. Bassaly after learning of my recent gynecological test results. Blood work is done and a CAT scan is taken, but guess what? Nothing shows up but the cyst on my right ovary, which we were already aware of. More negative tests. The doctors determine that my problem is caused from a flare up of my sciatic nerve. Steroids are prescribed and I'm sent home, relieved that my problem is not serious.

February, 2011

For a third time, Dr. Bassaly orders a CA 125 blood test. He performs a third Pap test and a third intravaginal sonogram. Those test results are clear. My CA 125 numbers, however, have been rising slightly with each test, but they are still in the normal range. I value his thoroughness, but my mind is racing ahead. At this point in the school year, I have a huge music program to prepare for that will be attended by over 400 community members! I don't have time for more appointments, I don't have time for waiting rooms, and I certainly don't have time for more tests! My health seems fine. Let's just chock things up to a fluke Pap smear back in August, okay?

Dr. Bassaly is still not satisfied. He calls me into his office after the great results of my February tests. He looks at me seriously, "Kim, I need to do a biopsy of your ovaries. The cyst is still there, and while it is not larger than before, it should be gone by now. I just want to make absolutely certain that I do not miss anything. I could not live with myself if I missed ovarian cancer. Something in my gut just tells me that I need to do this test. How about next Friday?"

I am silent for a moment. I want to be respectful, yet I don't feel the need for the biopsy. This will mean going to the hospital as an outpatient, being put under a general anesthetic and missing yet another day of work. How many tests must I go through before we decide that I'm okay? I have been through so many tests and I just don't have that gut feeling he is talking about. I'm healthy and fit. I walk at least three miles a day. What is all this fuss about? However, having great respect for my doctor, I will do whatever he asks me to do. If he feels more tests are needed, then I'll get more tests. Smiling at Dr. Bassaly, I politely say, "Next week is my music program..." He doesn't give up.

"The Friday after that, then."

He is not going to let me off the hook. I shrug my shoulders and say, "Sure." I don't have anything to lose; it will just be another test assuring me that all is well. Maybe then, we can drop this whole thing.

Two weeks later, the biopsy surgery is completed with no complications. As soon as I'm feeling better, a nurse wheels me out of the recovery room and back to where my husband is waiting for me. Rod sits down next to me. He looks quite calm. "Dr. Bassaly is pleased with what he saw. He thinks the ovaries look healthy. He said he took a little of each ovary for testing, and he flushed everything inside. He took a sampling from that fluid for testing, too."

The anesthetics have me feeling pretty groggy. I'm listening to Rod, but really have nothing much to say. I nod my head a little, letting him know his words are being heard. "Dr. Bassaly was smiling, Kim. I could tell he was happy with how things inside you look." Rod sighs, letting go a bit of his stress, he takes my hand, squeezes and says, "He told me that from what he saw, he *thinks* everything is okay."

"Good," I say. "Maybe now I am finished with all of these tests!" Grogginess takes over and I fall asleep.

March 1, 2011

Here I am, back at work, just four days after my biopsy, with a haunting message on my cell phone. What am I supposed to do? I don't have time to run down to the doctor's office *and* be at school for the parent night. What is so important that Dr. Bassaly needs me to come down now? Didn't he say that everything appeared to be all right after my biopsy? Now it's my turn to have that bad gut feeling. When a doctor places a phone call to me, asking me to come see him that same day, intuition kicks in and tells me that something is wrong.

I call Dr. Bassaly's office and talk with the receptionist. "Look, we have nearly one hundred parents and students arriving here at the school. Would you please ask Dr. Bassaly why he needs to see me right away? If it's not a big deal, can I just stop in tomorrow? If it's bad news, however, I want to know now. I don't want to be up all night worrying about what he's going to tell me." The nurse is kind and says to hold on, that she will be right back.

She returns to the phone and says softly, "Kim, Dr. Bassaly said you should stop down now."

There it is. I know. In that split second, my life and the lives of those who love me, are about to change. I'm calm, yet I know what he is going to tell me. One of my dearest friends, Ali, is standing nearby and she has heard the entire conversation. She looks at me, also understanding what I am about to face. "Do you want me to ride with you, Kim? You shouldn't be alone."

"No, it's fine. I'll be fine, really. Just let the other teachers know where I went, okay? I doubt if I'll be back for the math night event. Tell everyone I'm really sorry." She gives me a hug and offers again to ride along. Ali is like a daughter to me, and I'm thankful God placed her by my door at the exact moment of the call. I needed a hug, and she was there to give it. Once more, I tell Ali I'm fine. I jump in the car, turn on my K-Love Christian radio station, and head on to receive the news that has taken us seven months to finally discover – I have ovarian cancer.

⁂ ⁂ ⁂ ⁂ ⁂ ⁂

My husband, Rod, works from a home office, yet often must travel to inspect job sites. On this day, I know he had an out-of-town appointment. I call the house after leaving the school on my way to the doctor's, just to see if he might be home from his business trip. He is, so I quickly share with him what I think Dr. Bassaly is going to tell me. He wants to meet me at the doctor's office, but I tell him to just be waiting for me when I get home.

My meeting with Dr. Bassaly is brief. I know what he is going to tell me. I don't even cry, because at this point, the news does not surprise me. Ten miles of prayer on my way to the doctor's office gives me the strength I need to hear this diagnosis and accept it. Dr. Bassaly feels pretty certain the cancer is in an early stage, possibly even precancerous. He asks me if I am okay. Hearing that the doctor feels my cancer was found early makes it easy for me to remain calm. "I'll be okay, but first can we talk about my daughter?" Concern for Kaycee, my pregnant daughter, outweighs my concern for myself. This is my chance to talk to the doctor about my daughter's horrible nausea during her first trimester of pregnancy with our first grandchild. No medicine that she has tried seems to be helping so *Mama Bear* wants to see if she can help. After all, I truly feel fine, the seriousness of me having cancer is not really hitting home yet.

Doctor Bassaly rests his chin in his hand. "We can give her pills to help her nausea. Just have her call."

I persist. "Actually, if you are willing to give me the prescription now I would be happy to deliver it to her."

"Of course, I can do that for you." He smiles that wide, bright smile he has, and I feel relieved. Kaycee might possibly feel better tonight.

I take the script, give Dr. Bassaly a hug and ask him what *my* next steps are. Now that I have my daughter taken care of, I can ask him questions about myself. Dr. Bassaly refers me to Dr. Segreti in Pittsburgh at West Penn Hospital. She specializes in gynecologic oncology and is a recognized authority in the treatment of ovarian cancer. Dr. Bassaly's office will arrange for an appointment with her the following week. I'm now ready to start this new, unexpected, unwanted journey.

✐ ✐ ✐ ✐ ✐ ✐

During my drive home, I begin to process what the doctor has just told me. As I pull into the garage, Rod is there waiting, just as I asked him to be. The first tears come in a slow trickle. "We promised in sickness and in health, right? Well... I'm pretty sick." Rod opens up those strong, muscular arms of his and wraps them around me tightly. As I sink into his chest, he reassures me that we definitely made that promise to each other and that with God's strength we will get through this together.

Even as a teenager, Rod knew how to help me through trials. We first met shortly after my parents divorced. This was during the 70s when divorce was not such a common occurrence and considered by many to be shameful. Rod quickly noticed that my father was never around when he visited me. In my youthful immaturity, I was embarrassed to tell him my parents were divorced. When he discovered the truth, those same arms wrapped me in a teenage hug and whispered, "It's fine. Both your parents love you very much, I'm sure. It makes no difference to me."

In my late teens, these same arms held me when I returned home from seven months as an exchange student in Feldkirchen, Austria. I was an emotional mess. My grandfather had just passed away suddenly, and I was suffering from acute cystic acne (it required over fifty shots to heal it). Rod wrapped those big arms around me and reminded me of eternal life. "You will see your grandfather again. He is in heaven. *And*... you are still very beautiful to me, despite what your skin is going through." To a teenage girl, those words meant the world.

There have been many other trials over the years when Rod's arms have held me and assured me that we would get through our troubles together. Today is no different. We stand for several minutes in our garage holding each other. Rod reminds me, once again, that we will get through this illness. That is all I need to hear. Enough crying. I will be strong. I need to be strong for myself and all of those who love me.

That evening we decide we must tell our two daughters of my diagnosis. First, we set off to my oldest daughter's house. Kaycee is my artistic, free-spirited and very sensitive child, so I worry how this news will affect her. She and her husband, Tim, are expecting our first grandchild, Trenton Patrick, at the beginning of October. I hate to burden her with additional stress as she is feeling so poorly, but I'm also excited to get to her house because in my hand is a prescription from Dr. Bassaly to help her feel better.

After the initial chit-chat about the weather and school, I say to Kaycee, "Do you remember, honey, that Dr. Bassaly has been giving me all sorts of tests since August?" Immediately, she shows signs of nervousness. She knows something is coming.

"Yes..." she answers. "What's wrong, Mom?"

Oh, she's good, I think. My intuition is pretty good, but Kaycee's is even more in tune. "Well, today he told me that I have ovarian cancer." Her tears begin before all of my words are out of my mouth. "Kaycee... it will be okay. Dr. Bassaly says that we caught it early. I'm going to see a specialist in Pittsburgh and everything will be fine."

"No, it's not, Mom. You're just telling me this, aren't you? Ovarian cancer is never okay." Kaycee is sobbing uncontrollably. "You're not going to be fine, are you?"

Seeing my child's anguish is hard. I wish she did not have to have a mother who is sick. But I am so grateful it is I who am sick and not her that I whisper a prayer of thanksgiving. *"Lord, thank You that it is me who has this disease. Please spare my girls from ever receiving this diagnosis in their lifetime."*

After further discussion with Kaycee, we leave her in Tim's capable hands. He will continue to comfort her, as they both learn to accept this. How fortunate Rod and I are to have two good young men in our daughters' lives. We head up to Grove City College to let my youngest daughter know what's going on. In this day and age of Facebook and Twitter, I'm afraid somehow she may find out through the internet about my condition before I have a chance to tell her myself, so we make the trip to Grove City that night.

During Nicolette's baby and toddler years, there was a period of time when Rod's job required an extreme amount of travel and time away from home. Because of this, Nicolette developed an unusually close bond to me. The news of my cancer, while difficult for everyone, may be especially tough on her. She always wears her heart on her sleeve.

On the way, I call her boyfriend, Luke, and ask if he can come with us to talk to Nicolette in her dorm lobby. Since Nicolette and Luke are in a serious relationship, I know it's best if Luke is with her when we tell her about my cancer. She'll need his strong presence to help her through this. When we arrive, we text Nicolette to let her know we are there. She's excited, because it's rare that

Rod and I show up in the middle of the week. She comes bouncing out to the lobby, her pony tail swishing back and forth, all smiles. We embrace in a big hug.

"Hey! What are all of you doing here?"

My stomach does a slow, sickly churn at the thought of what I'm going to tell her. I wish I could just say, "Surprise! We're taking you and Luke to the Main Street Diner for burgers!" That will have to wait for another time. "Well, we have something we want to talk to both of you about, so we drove up to see you." We sit in the lobby, and I begin to recite the same words I shared with Kaycee and Tim an hour earlier. There is something devastating in just saying the word *cancer*. I avoid it at all costs, but at this time it needs to be said.

Nicolette immediately puts her face into her hands and begins to cry. Luke shows his strength in that moment by taking control. I'm so proud of him and the man he is showing himself to be. He calmly asks if he can pray for us right then and there. We all join hands and Luke prays. I have a peace within me that only comes through prayer. Our strong faith in Christ, and the love and support of my family and friends, will carry me through the days ahead.

 శారీ శారీ శారీ శారీ శారీ శారీ

After an evening of processing the reality of my illness, I'm ready to fight it. When a free moment arises at school the next morning, I am on the phone calling Dr. Bassaly's office, "Uhh, yes, I am wondering if Dr. Bassaly had a chance to call Dr. Segreti's office yet to get me an appointment?"

"Hold on a minute while I check, please." Silence for a few minutes and the receptionist is back. "Dr. Bassaly actually did talk to Dr. Segreti this morning, Kim. Their office is waiting for your call."

Okay, I'm impressed that Dr. Bassaly is on top of my case. On the other hand, it's now up to me to call Pittsburgh, and that means things are going to get serious. My appointment with Dr. Segreti is scheduled for the next Monday. Meanwhile, I am told to go to our local hospital to get scans done, and that I will need to bring the results to the appointment.

Today is the day for my scans. I have to consume an awful thick, white liquid before arriving at the hospital – one quart at noon and another quart one hour before my scan. Not wanting to miss work again, I make my appointment for the end of the day. The first quart of the white liquid is fine. I forego the lunchroom and eat in the privacy of my classroom. However, the second quart is going to be trickier.

Five young boys are working on a reading program at the computers. Somehow I've got to drink this disgusting concoction while still teaching these students. I assist them, sneak behind the book shelves, squat down where they cannot see me, plug my nose and take a swallow. After about ten of these runs between the boys and the bookshelves, the drink is finally finished. It's amazing, the boys never have a clue their teacher is silently gagging and about to cry. In the end, I step out with a smile on my face and chirp, "You boys are doing such a fantastic job!" and I think to myself, I am too.

While waiting for the week to pass until I will see Dr. Segreti, I go to work each day as if nothing has changed. It's easy for me to do this, because anyone who is a primary teacher knows that our days are never idle. In fact, we barely have time to get to the restroom, let alone sit around thinking about being sick. One of my co-workers, Anita, is busy in the first grade pod area. Our eyes meet as I walk by.

She smiles and says, "You're wearing our color."

Confused and having no idea what she's talking about, I ask, "Our color? What do you mean?"

"Teal. It stands for ovarian cancer. Pink is breast cancer." Anita rushes by on her way to her next task. Over her shoulder she calls, "You look good in teal."

For a moment, I stand dumbfounded. This is the first time I am made aware that each type of cancer has a different color representing it. Hmmph, she is right. Teal is one of my favorite colors. If I have to go down this path, at least teal is a great color to wear. Then I remember how Anita had ovarian cancer six years ago. Another teacher's aide in our building, Marjorie, is off work with breast cancer. Just two weeks ago, the staff sat together in the school library as the news of her illness was shared with all of us. Little did I know that I would be next...the three of us now share a bond that none of us would choose, but which somehow has chosen us.

✍ ✍ ✍ ✍ ✍ ✍

Monday comes quickly. Rod drives me to West Penn Hospital in Pittsburgh for my appointment. The nurses are especially friendly and make me feel as relaxed as possible. Everyone is complimenting me on how thin I am. In the past six months, my weight has dropped by eight pounds. I kind of like being this thin, too, but I'm just now realizing the true reason for my weight loss.

Dr. Segreti comes into the office definitely in command. I like that. If someone is going to cut me open and save my life, the doctor needs to be someone who has confidence.

"So, where is this really nice lady from New Castle I'm hearing about?" she asks.

I guess she means me? Must be Dr. Bassaly talking about me, I think to myself. I laugh and answer all of the doctor's questions as she examines me both internally and externally. "No, I don't have any pain there...No, I don't feel extra tired...No, that does not hurt." The words *silent killer* keep running through my mind.

Maybe I should be terribly afraid, but at this point there are no feelings of fear. The diagnosis just doesn't seem real to me yet. It's hard to believe you are sick when you feel fine, maybe even better than fine. I feel great. Yes, exhaustion hits me at the end of the day, but what teacher is not tired when she gets home?

After my exam, Rod and I meet with Dr. Segreti and her assistants. She explains the surgery and says that she has me scheduled for Wednesday. My mouth drops open as I look at Rod. His face also shows surprise. "Do you mean *this* Wednesday?" My voice reveals my shock.

"Yep." Dr. Segreti looks at me very matter-of-factly, as if she does not expect me to be surprised by a surgery date scheduled only two days from today.

"Wow, okay, I guess. May as well get it out of me as soon as possible, right?" I cannot even say the word cancer. I hate that word. I just call my sickness *it*.

"There is always a chance once we get in there that you may need to have blood. You will need to sign papers that this is okay with you." Dr. Segreti turns and nods to the nurse to get the necessary paperwork.

For some reason, this bothers me. Maybe it is from my younger years when people got AIDS and other diseases through blood transfusions, but this news scares me. "Can't I have his blood?" I point to Rod. "He is O, the universal donor." Unfortunately, there is not enough time for Rod's blood to be taken and saved for me. The doctor can tell this bothers me, but I sign the papers. What choice do I have? She explains that chemotherapy will be used as a follow-up treatment starting approximately six weeks to two months after the surgery. "Do you mean the kind of chemo where your hair falls out? Am I going to lose my hair?"

Dr. Segreti looks me straight in the eye. "Yes, you will."

Disbelief sets in. From my meeting with Dr. Bassaly, I didn't think my case was so serious. Wasn't *it* stage I, possibly even pre-cancerous? Wrong. The scans show otherwise.

"Your cancer is most likely early stage III, but we can't be sure until we get in there. Most patients I see are much further along than you. This type of cancer is very aggressive, so we will treat it aggressively right back."

There is a moment of quiet. So much information in such a short amount of time. *Overwhelmed* is the perfect word to describe how I'm feeling. There's no sense in wasting any more time. "Ok, then let's do it." We make the plans for Wednesday. As the doctor is leaving the room, I'm thinking, I just met this woman forty-five minutes ago and in two days she will be slicing me open. How do

I really feel about that? As she is just about to leave the room I call out, "Doctor Segreti!" She stops and turns around.

She raises an eyebrow. "Yes?"

"You *are* good, right?"

Without a moment's hesitation, a smile lights her face and she fires back, "Oh, I'm *very* good." We laugh, and I feel relief.

"Good. That's what I wanted to hear." Our eyes connect, and I know that we share a respect for one another. She is the doctor I need. Between her and The Great Healer, I will be all right.

వా వా వా వా వా వా

It is Tuesday, the day before my surgery. I spend the day drinking some awful lemonade concoction that empties me, causing me to now be yet another several pounds lighter. Text messages fill up my phone throughout the day. Family and friends wish me well and offer up their prayers on my behalf.

Reading literature on ovarian cancer passes the hours. In these pamphlets, I learn of the symptoms I had, but never realized: weight loss, pelvic pressure when I was on the treadmill, some constipation and a reduced appetite. The most current saying for o.c. (sorry, I hate the words ovarian cancer, remember?) is that o.c. whispers. I must be completely deaf, then. I did not hear it whisper, not even a tiny whoosh of breath. When all of this is over, my platform will be making others aware of this *whispering illness*. My prayer is that others do not have to discover *it*, when it is too late.

My eyes are burning at this point from the non-stop reading of every ovarian cancer pamphlet put to press. Rod tells me to take a break. He will read the information and tell me if he learns anything new. Just looking at the literature makes me want to scoop it all up, trash it and pretend none of this is really happening. At times, this is how I handle my illness, as if it's not real.

Standing in front of our bedroom mirror, I pull up my pajama top and take one last look at my flat stomach with no marks. Breathing deeply, I gently run my right hand across my abdomen, knowing that a 10 inch incision will be there by this time tomorrow evening. Pills are lined up for me on the counter just waiting for their time to be swallowed. I am a person who refuses to take medicine unless there is no other option. Well, there is no other option. The pills go down, and I climb into bed. The phone rings. It's my mother calling from Florida.

"How are you doing, honey?"

At the sound of her voice, tears well up in my eyes. Last week she was ready to fly here for the surgery, but I told her no, she would be more helpful afterwards. "I'm fine. I just want it all to be over with." Now I'm thinking that I need her here. Why didn't I ask her to come home?

"You know that we're praying for you. You're young and strong; everything is going to be all right. We were reading about Dr. Segreti on the internet. Looks like you're in good hands."

Sliding down the side of the bed, I sit on the floor. "Yea, I like her."

"I wish I was there. I should be there with you."

I hear Mom's wish in her voice. It's probably best she's not here, though, because there's something about my mother, and my husband, that makes me cry. In their presence, I feel as if someone else is sharing this burden and trying to solve my problem. When they're around, I don't have to be the one in control. Even as a fifty year old woman, the next time I see my mom, I will cry. "Rod has your number. He'll call you as soon as my surgery is over. Okay? I love you!"

"I love you, too, honey." Click. I wish she was here.

I'm scheduled for nine o'clock. The nurse told us to plan on two and a half to three hours of surgery. People from New York to Florida and California are praying for me. I can actually feel a peace. Those prayers are giving me strength and comfort.

Both of my daughters call and ask to come with us to Pittsburgh. I tell them no, that they can come visit afterward. Nana and Aunt Tammy will be there all day with their dad. Protecting my girls from the ugliness of this disease is important to me. This isn't an appendix operation or a tooth extraction. My daughters don't need to see me come out of surgery with tubes sticking out of me, an oxygen mask on my face, and looking close to death. They are already handling enough.

Our dear friend and leader from church, Pastor John Yergan, will also be with Rod to offer his support throughout the day. Pastor John's prayers have such a calming effect on me. I hope that I'm able to see him before surgery.

Late in the evening, the door into our kitchen opens and who is there? It's Nicolette. She arranged to miss her classes tomorrow so that she can come with us to Pittsburgh. I am touched but not pleased. She has such a tender heart, and I worry how she will handle the stress of tomorrow.

Kaycee will likely be upset that she is now the only one not coming in the morning, but she needs to only worry about herself and her little baby, my grandson, growing inside of her. Despite this ordeal before me, just knowing that I will be a grandmother soon is such an inspiration for me to fight through all of this.

2

Surgery

March 16, 2011

It is five o'clock in the morning when my alarm goes off. Why do they do this to people? Not only does one have to go through surgery, but they always schedule it so early that you are up before the sun. Anyone who knows me knows that I believe mankind should only awaken once it is light outside! Oh, well, I'll be sleeping all day anyway. Because of the sleeping pill I took, it's hard for me to wake up and get ready. God love my husband, my personal chauffeur. This is the first of many trips to Pittsburgh the man will make on my behalf... and always with a positive outlook and a smile to give me strength.

We arrive at the hospital and don't have to wait long before it's my turn to go in and be prepped for surgery. I wait in the pre-surgery room, reciting several of the scripture verses Luke's mom, Hope, has shared with me for encouragement. She knows the scriptures, and helps me find those I can call on when needing strength. At this time my favorite is:

> *Don't worry about anything, instead pray about every-*
> *thing... tell God what you need and thank Him for all*
> *He has done... if you do this, you will experience God's*
> *peace which is far more wonderful than the human mind*
> *can understand... His peace will guard your hearts and*
> *minds as you live in Christ Jesus.*
> Philippians 4:6-7 (NLW)

I make posters of this verse for each of my girls to read when they need comfort. Another poster is put on the wall of my hospital room. This verse will keep Rod strong, as well as share our faith with those who visit and take care of me. Until Rod and Nicolette are allowed back with me, I snuggle into the pillow and close my eyes. I imagine Jesus wrapping His arms around me. He holds me and allows me to feel a peace beyond understanding. Like a father, He comforts me, his hurting child.

Though I am lying down, my legs are still sideways. I have my tennis shoes on and don't want to put my shoes on the bed. So far, no hospital slippers have arrived, so I'm really not sure what to do. My mother has engrained good manners into me since childhood. I cannot imagine putting my shoes on the bed. A young intern stops at my bed.

"How are you doing, Mrs. McCormick?"

"I'm fine." I smile, wanting to be positive throughout this experience. "I'm just not sure what to do with my feet. I want to lie down, but I don't want to take off my shoes."

The intern pats the end of my bed. "It's a hospital bed," she says matter-of-factly. "That's what it's for. Put them up here."

Relieved and feeling much more comfortable now, I realize how silly, that under these circumstances, my greatest worry was about putting my shoes on top of the hospital bed! Finally, Rod and Nicolette come back. They give me hugs and kisses before Dr. Segreti shows up. Within minutes, she arrives.

"Are you ready?" She speaks with encouragement in her voice. I need that.

"Let's get this show over with," I say. After a final kiss from Rod and Nicolette, the medical team walks me back to the operating room.

I'm standing outside the door to surgery with two interns. I want to know them better. I want them to know me better. "Why did you girls go into medicine? What made you want to be doctors?" They appear surprised that I'm asking *them* questions right before my major surgery. Do they think I'm strange, wanting to have a conversation at this time, minutes before my intestines will be lying upon my stomach while the doctor carves me out like a pumpkin? But I need to establish at least a hint of personal connection; for them to know I am more than just a body on which to practice their surgery skills. Both doctors tell me they have known since childhood they wanted to help make people well. Their conviction reassures me. I share with them that teaching is my calling and what a rewarding job it is to help little children learn to read. I tell them I'm married to a wonderful man, have two beautiful children, and will be a grandmother soon. There, enough said.

My special verse chosen to lead me through this moment plays over and over again in my head.

Be strong and courageous. Do not be terrified; do not be discouraged, for the Lord your God will be with you wherever you go.

Joshua 1:9 (NIV)

Once in the surgical room, my brain gives me short, robotic commands to follow. Walk to the table. Crawl onto the bed. Listen to the anesthesiologist. As soon as the medication is connected to me, muddled thoughts begin gathering into brain clouds. She looks nice. I get so sick. Please help me not get sick. Count to 10? She is pretty. Please, not too... much... medicine. And I am out.

∽∽∽∽∽∽

My family sits in the waiting room while I am in surgery. According to Rod, the time spent waiting was grueling. After the expected three hours go by, a nurse comes to talk to my family.

"The surgery is going well. Your wife is fine. The doctor is being very cautious and taking her time to do the job right. It will be awhile longer, but we will keep you posted."

As quickly as she arrived, the nurse is gone. Another hour and a half goes by. Rod is beginning to worry, yet understands the complexity of what is going on. Nicolette is not quite as understanding.

"Dad, *what* are they doing? Something must be wrong! They said it would take three hours max, we're at four and a half! You need to find out what's going on!"

Putting his arm around our daughter, he tries to calm her. She is anxious and on the verge of tears, imagining the worst. "These are the times when our faith is all we have, Nic. It's okay to cry, we're all worried. Just keep the faith, Kiddo."

Kaycee is calling and texting Nicolette continuously throughout the day, wanting updates and struggling through the slowly passing minutes, as she waits for news. Being at work, rather than with the rest of the family, is difficult for her. I still believe it was best, though, that she did not witness my immediate release from this major surgery.

Rod decides to call back to the nurses' station and ask for an update. He is told, once again, that everything is fine; things are just taking a little longer than anticipated. Finally, after six and a half hours, the surgery is over. The nurse appears again.

"Your wife is doing fine. She's in recovery right now. Dr. Segreti will be here to speak with you, as soon as possible."

Forty-five minutes later, Dr. Segreti comes out. Rod calls her the "Italian angel." She may not even be Italian, but she appears to be, and it's a great nickname.

With her usual confidence she says, "The cancer was bad, but I feel 99% sure that I got it all!"

Now Nicolette allows her tears of joy and relief to flow.

Dr. Segreti explains that my cancer was stage IIIc, stage four being the most advanced. My cervix, uterus, omentum, ovaries, and two lymph nodes were removed. Determined that she would not need to give me blood, she spent over two hours removing a single lymph node that was wrapped around a main artery.

Later, Dr. Segreti's intern tells us that she has never worked with a doctor as meticulous as Dr. Segreti. We are blessed.

∽∽∽∽∽∽

I wake in my hospital room to the sound of Rod's voice talking with the nurses. Surprisingly, I *think* my body is feeling fine, no pain. The nurses try to move me from the transport bed to the bed in the room. That is when I understand what just happened to me. The pain I feel from my stomach wound is unbearable, and out comes a blood-curdling scream. They stop just long enough for me to take a few deep breaths. Tears are pouring down my face. The nurses try to move me again. As much as I don't want to yell, I can't help it. Despite the grogginess and medication throughout my body, I hear myself screaming. They stop once again.

"On a scale of one to ten, what would you call this pain, Kim?" The nurse is concerned.

"Eleven." I am still crying.

The nurses are bustling about the room. Rod is by my side asking me if there is any way he can help me. Clutching his hand, I tell him the pain is unbearable.

The intern on duty orders a type of support band to wrap around my middle. While the nurses tend to putting this on me, my body is rolled side to side. I scream again. "I cannot bear this, Rod. I cannot bear the pain."

"Is it like childbirth, Kim?" a nurse asks.

"Worse." I'm breathing with difficulty and feel as if I may pass out. Perhaps that would be better. Then they can move me, and I won't know what's going on. A nurse places a button in my hand.

"When we lift you, push this button. It's morphine, and it will help you get through the pain."

The support band helps tremendously, but it's the morphine that gets me through.

Our initial plans for the week were for Rod to spend his nights at a hotel just down the block from the hospital. Now that he sees the condition I'm in, he cancels his reservations and sets up camp in my room. He doesn't leave the hospital for five days, while he takes care of me. Good men may be hard to find, but I have one. God blessed me with Rod's love. I don't think that I can love Rod more than I already do, but this experience shows me that it's possible for a great love to become greater.

Over the next five days, my body sleeps and heals. Each day is progress. First, the catheter is removed. Next, the oxygen. I sleep, and then sleep some more. As soon as I awake, I reach for Rod's hand. Whether it's daytime, or in the middle of the night, it is always there.

By the fourth day, they bring me solid food, but all Rod can get me to eat are potato chips. It is strange; I began craving potato chips while I was ill but did not yet know I was sick. This craving for potato chips will last for a couple of months. For now, chips are all that taste good to me. On Saturday, I finally eat half of a hamburger.

Rod is thankful that the college basketball finals are on. There is a decent television in the room, and he spends hours tending to my needs and watching the games. I'm happy about this, too, because I'm already feeling guilty about everything he has to do for me. Becoming a burden is not acceptable. Basketball is Rod's favorite sport, so this eases some of my guilt.

My sisters, Rhonda and Jamie, Luke's parents, as well as Kaycee and Tim, come to visit me the second day. Though still heavily medicated, I know who they are. The drugs have me pretty sedated; life seems to be moving in slow motion. I remember reaching my hand out and grasping through the air all around my face. My visitors are laughing. Finally, Rod asks, "Kim what are you doing?"

"Trying to scratch my nose! I can't find it!" My hand keeps feeling around my face.

"Let me help you!" Rod comes and puts my hand on my nose.

This is pretty funny, but I can't laugh. It will only make my stomach hurt, and then I will need to push my morphine button. I hate medicine, so I'm trying not to use it anymore.

The hospital room where I'm staying is cozy and comforting. The soft blue decor makes me feel relaxed. Even the floor is a warm Pergo-like wood, rather than the cold tile typically found in hospitals. This part of the hospital was recently remodeled, so everything about the room appears new. The fact that no one else shares the room with us is a bonus. Rod is able to shower right in my room and sleep on the recliner. It's pretty uncomfortable for a guy who is six foot one, but he manages and never complains. He's not sure if he is really supposed to use the bathroom and shower in my room, but there's no other choice, and no one tells him otherwise. All of the staff is wonderful. We have no complaints about West Penn Hospital.

I've heard that anesthetics are like a truth serum. Ask a person under the influence of this medication questions, and you will hear only truthful answers. Those around me are amazed when my conversation after surgery is about the angel who watched over my operation. There was an angel at my side. I don't remember this, but Rod says that I insisted that an angel watched over my entire surgery. Experiencing a peace like I have never known, especially in such a stressful situation, helps me to be certain that God sent an angel my way to give me comfort.

Several times a day Rod takes me for walks around the hallway. We walk to the big windows near the elevators and look out across a Pittsburgh neighborhood. There's an old stone church in my view. I'd like to visit there and pray for my health, family and friends inside of that old church's walls. Instead, my prayers are sent heavenward, staring out at the church from the sixth floor window.

When Saturday arrives, it's time for my first shower in four days. Fabulous. The water gently pelts my body for so long that Rod is concerned.

"Are you okay in there? What's taking you so long?"

The water is massaging every inch of my body, (every inch except for my incision, of course). "Sorry it's taking me so long, but I'm experiencing heaven on earth!"

As the warm water flows over me, I imagine all the cancer cells seeping out of me and flowing along with the water down the drain, as far away as they can go. A small gasp escapes me, as I see myself in the mirror for the first time in four days. My eyebrows need to be shaped, my hair looks crazy, and I am lily pale. I immediately ask for make-up, a brush, and some tweezers.

My appearance doesn't need to suffer so, now that I'm feeling much better.

Rod is surprised with my improved look and tells me how beautiful I am. This is the first of many times he reminds me of his love, knowing that I need to hear these words. What makes them so special is that he really means them. We are now at a point in our relationship where beauty is found inside of us, not on the outside. Who has not been told at least once in their lifetime that what really matters is what's inside? As teenagers we scoff at the remark, but as adults, you realize how true these words are.

3

Beginning to Heal

By Sunday morning, I am allowed to go home. Rod says,
"I hope you're not upset with me. I know you told your mother
that she didn't need to come up from Florida to be with you, but
I called her anyway. I asked her to come home to help you and
me. I don't know how you feel about that, but I did it. I think she
needs to be here."

I'm not upset at all, but don't want to be a burden on anyone,
especially my mom. She loves the Florida weather and the sun,
which she won't find in western Pennsylvania. Who wants to
leave Florida and come to Western Pennsylvania in March? No
one in their right mind, I am thinking. It's not long after we are
home that Rhonda arrives with Mom in tow. She picked Mom up
at the airport. Slowly, I make my way across the floor, thrilled to
see her. We embrace in a long awaited hug. It's always a relief to
have your mom around when you're sick. I think that the worst

is behind me now. All I need to do is recover from surgery and things will be much better. We are all very naïve. There is much more to come.

Rod needs to get back to work. His employer has been very understanding this past week, but business goes on, and he needs to be involved. Fortunately, he has a home office from which to work, but he also must travel to the sites of the construction projects which he manages. Now, with my mother here, he will be able to travel as needed.

At first, I need someone to bend down and wrap their arms under my shoulders to help me stand from a seated position. In the mornings, Mom has to bend over to lift me up from bed. Then I'm able to swing my legs around and stand for myself. It's amazing how each day shows improvement. For exercise, I shuffle slowly around the rooms of our house. As soon as I can comfortably go down steps, I talk my mother into letting me go on the treadmill, but this is not an easy win.

"Kimberly." Mom uses my full name when she means business. "I'll let you walk on that treadmill, if you promise to go at a safe speed."

Have we traveled back to my teenage years? Ha, ha! "I'm not going to go too fast, Mom. I don't want to rip something open and go back into the hospital. I'll be careful." She comes down the steps with me and folds laundry while I poke along at turtle speed.

"Are you sure that thing can't go slower, Kimberly Ann?" Her eyebrows raise, giving me that *mother* look we children know so well.

"I feel like I'm crawling, Mom!"

"Just see if it can go slower, it seems a little fast." She waits for me to push the button to adjust the speed.

"I'm telling you, Mom, it doesn't go any slower."

"Okay, I hear you. Just prove it to me."

Guess what? It does go slower. Why are mothers always right?

∽∽∽∽∽∽

One particular morning the sun comes shining through the draperies. Could it really be true? In Western Pennsylvania, we do not see the sun often and it's been a long winter. That sunshine peeking through my window gives me the boost I need. I'm out of bed and dressed, ready to take a drive. "Mom, the sun is out! Let's get out of the house! I just want to see the sunshine." My mother is all for it. We gather our things and go to the garage. Mom is driving my car when we go anywhere, so I ride shotgun.

"Where do you want to go?" she asks.

"Anywhere. I can't pass up this gorgeous morning sitting inside the house."

We enjoy the clear skies, sunshine, and signs of spring. Mom drives through Dunkin' and buys me a decaf coffee. This is quite a treat. After driving around the township, we head for home. What a revived attitude I have simply from being outside in God's world.

∽∽∽∽∽∽

Each morning, Mom and I hold devotions together before breakfast. This is a special time for us. Both of us understand that it is our great God who ultimately holds our lives in His hands. Doubt has no place in my mind when thinking of my future health. There are just too many things I feel called to do on this Earth. Restored health requires my complete focus.

After taking my medicines, I lie on the couch for Mom to give me my daily stomach injection. The medicine helps prevent blood clots. Once I start feeling better, Mom teaches me how to do this for myself: With a cotton ball soaked in rubbing alcohol, I dab a spot on my stomach. Next, I disinfect the needle in the same way. The hardest part is actually sticking the needle into my stomach. Now the meaning of the Nike slogan, "Just do it!" makes sense. Speed is the answer here. Before long, I'm a pro! This goes on for weeks until the large container of syringes are all gone. Each time an obstacle on my journey back to health is finished, I celebrate. Hooray! No more stomach shots!

Our house is flooded with cards, flowers and meals sent in by friends and co-workers. One day the postman tells Rod that he is relieved to see him. With so many cards coming to me, the floral truck in the driveway so often, and Rod's car never leaving the house for days, he was afraid that Rod has passed on! That gives all of us a good laugh.

෴ ෴ ෴ ෴ ෴ ෴

At a post-surgery follow-up appointment with Dr. Segreti, we discuss having my blood tested for the BRCA1 and BRCA2 genes. "The vast majority of hereditary breast and ovarian cancer is due to an alteration or mutation in either the BRCA1 or BRCA2 genes. These mutations can be inherited from either your mother or father" (Hereditary Breast and Ovarian Cancer Syndrome pamphlet, 2010). This information can be diagnosed through a simple blood test.

Learning that my test results are negative is a thrill not only to me, but my entire family of women. A positive test result would mean that my mother, sisters and daughters are also at risk. In fact, women who carry this gene are recommended to have their ovaries removed after age thirty-five as a preventative measure. A family sigh of relief is shared among us.

Quite often I wonder how my cancer started in the first place. Are there changes I should make in my lifestyle to help prevent cancer from reoccurring in my future? Family history plays a part. My paternal grandparents both died of cancer in their late 40s and early 50s. My father had colon cancer in his early 50s. My maternal grandmother had cancer in her 70s. Now you understand why I am concerned about my genetics. I'm searching for any answers. Without a cause, it doesn't make sense. So many times I've read or heard about stress playing a part in cancer. Stress places humans at risk for many types of illnesses. Could that have been a factor in my case?

Thinking back upon the past year, I realize the tremendous stress of all that happened. To begin with, my stepmother of thirty two years passed away, leaving my elderly father alone and struggling with her absence. During the summer months, I drove thirty minutes five days a week to Dad's home and spent the day with him. Rhonda and Jamie took care of the weekends and some evenings, but as a teacher I had the long summer vacation, which my sisters did not. Ultimately, we had to close up the house that my father and stepmother had shared all those years and relocate

Dad into a near-by assisted living apartment where he would be comfortable and happy.   In addition, Nicolette had graduated from high school that June and was preparing for college in the fall. I needed to spend time with her and help prepare for the next chapter of her life, as well as the next chapter of ours—the empty nest. It was stressful, trying to balance my time with Dad and my time with my own family.

Then, our beautiful collie, Bella, had to be put down in August. She was a loyal family member for thirteen years. She was also the only family member who really enjoyed listening to me play the piano! I'm not very good, but Bella would lie down next to the piano and camp out there for my *recital.*

So much was going on. I thought I was handling everything well. It's easy to see how a woman misses the *whispers.* My symptoms of weight loss, pelvic pressure, some constipation, and a reduced appetite, were easily explained away by the circumstances of any given day. Will I ever learn what pulled the "cancer trigger?" It's doubtful. Lifestyle is important, but I was already making wise daily health choices. Life is not always in our control. I have surrendered my concerns about becoming sick again over to my Lord. Without this faith and trust in my Lord my worry of a possible recurrence would drive me crazy!

୬ஒ ୬ஒ ୬ஒ ୬ஒ ୬ஒ ୬ஒ

Teal bracelets arrive in the mail from my niece, Lisa. There is one for each family member. We all plan to wear these until my chemo treatments are over. This is just one of many thoughtful actions from my family and friends.

When my friend, Marjorie, became ill, we teachers created a *meal calendar* where groups of us signed up to take turns providing her family with meals. I quickly learn that the teachers decide to make double the food and add my name to the meal calendar. Every Thursday, Rod and I receive delicious meals from my co-workers. Other days, my sisters and friends bring food over. We have chicken noodle soup, vegetable soup, wedding soup, ham and bean soup, meatball soup, chili, and more chicken noodle soup. The food is absolutely delicious, but this abundance of soup spawns a running joke in the house. If there is a lull in the conversation...would anyone care for a bowl of soup? If you've got a minute to spare...would you like a bowl of soup? It's a cold winter, however, and every drop of soup is enjoyed. We are overwhelmed by the outpouring of love we receive.

Ali arrives one day after school with gifts in hand.

"What in the world do you have for me now, Ali?" I love Ali. She was a student teacher for me when she was in college. Now she is my co-worker.

"Well," she replies, "the staff got together and collected some money to buy you a present. You said you have a lot of time on your hands right now, and we know how much you love to read, so..."

My gift from the staff is a Kindle and cash. Tears flow as I express my gratitude to Ali. What fun to download a variety of books onto the Kindle. The money is tucked away for when my chemotherapy is finished. It will be a costly appointment when my hair is ready for color treatment. Beyond any gifts the staff can give me, it is their kindness that touches my heart

⁓ ⁓ ⁓ ⁓ ⁓ ⁓

With each day, my strength increases. Climbing the mountain to recovery is not easy, and when the summit is reached, I want to stay there.   Unfortunately, while the surgery is behind me, my chemotherapy will start soon. Sliding back down that slope is not going to be fun. Understanding why I even have to go through chemo is difficult, especially when I feel well.

Choosing whether to receive my chemo in Pittsburgh or in New Castle is our first decision. Because I get car sick, the drive to and from the city when I'm already feeling nauseated from chemo is not appealing. Dr. Segreti tells me that it's fine to stay in New Castle. However, the advantage of West Penn Hospital is that they specialize in chemo for gynecological cancers. The nurses are trained in the delivery of chemo through an abdominal port. Rod and I do not need to discuss this very long. We are happy with my care at West Penn Hospital. He's willing to drive me to Pittsburgh for all of my treatments. We schedule a day in May for me to have a PICC line (peripherally inserted central catheter) put into my arm and a port for the chemo placed into my abdomen. I need to keep getting stronger and stronger, for what is coming next, is going to be the hardest part of my journey.

⁓ ⁓ ⁓ ⁓ ⁓ ⁓

My body is gaining strength, and I now feel confident enough to suggest that my mother return to Florida. She agrees. She decides to go back and close up the condo that she and Tom, my stepfather, live in and then head back to Pennsylvania. They will stay until my chemo is finished.

Before my chemo sessions begin I need to get myself strong again. The baby crawls my mom allowed me to do on the treadmill graduate to slow walks behind a grocery cart at the store with Rod. Finally, we are able to return to taking our after-supper walks. At first, we walk very slowly and for short distances.

A neighbor from across the street yells out, "Hey, we noticed you're going slower this year. Is everything okay?"

We take the time to chat and update him and his wife on the battle we are fighting. Despite living across the street from this couple for years, we have rarely spoken to each other, only sharing smiles and waves whenever our paths happened to cross. This day is the beginning of a new friendship. Over the next months we receive phone calls and cards from them. They always include a special Bible verse to offer us encouragement. Another example of how my illness is causing love to grow.

My birthday arrives in April. I thought age fifty was going to be the best year of my life so far. The start of it was certainly wonderful when Rod, Nicolette, Luke and I went to Florida to swim with the dolphins. This was in celebration of Nicolette's high school graduation and my fiftieth birthday. "Fifty is nifty," right? Hmmmmm, what happened? Now I am fifty-one. Life is going to get much worse before it gets better; thankfully, so many precious moments occur along the way.

This afternoon the mailbox is stuffed full of cards. How they all fit in the box is the mailman's secret. He happens to be just a house away, so he calls out, "Is everything okay at your house?" This overflow of cards must remind him of my surgery days.

"Nothing to worry about this time! It's my birthday, and I have a feeling that my friends have thrown a card shower on me!"

I sprint up the driveway, anxious to open every single card. I read each one with care, taking the time to soak up the kind words shared by so many of my friends and co-workers. The Wilmington Area School District is populated with a tremendous group of people. The administrators, teachers, aides, office workers, cafeteria, and custodial staff are the best. These friends and acquaintances are examples of how good people still prevail in our world today.

My in-laws, Janet and Wayne, visit to wish me a happy birthday. Rod's mom hands me a special present and says, "I thought you might enjoy something a little different this year." Their present to me is a beautiful angel with teal colored trim on the angel's gown. I understand the love put into this gift choice and smile.

"Thank you, Mom and Dad. I will always treasure this angel." Their love and thoughtfulness touches my soul.

"Wait, there's one more thing." Rod's dad heads outside, and we follow him. With great care, Dad unwraps an unusually shaped wooden creation. Dad is a talented woodworker. "I know how much you and Rod love to take care of your yard. This year it seemed like I should make you something a little extra special. I made you a butterfly house."

I clap my hands together. Butterflies remind me of peace, such gentle creatures. "I love it! I know just where we can put it!" The small island in our yard is just perfect for this new lawn ornament. Dad places the butterfly house among the cedar chips. We all step back and admire his handiwork.

"Thank you so much, Dad. You certainly did not need to do this... but I'm glad you did!"

Dad gives me a hug and says, "It should have been me." I understand what he is saying, but I ask him anyway.

"What do you mean by that?"

"You shouldn't be the one going through this. I'm already old. You kids have your whole lives ahead of you. It should be me, not you."

Tears come to my eyes, but I reassure Dad that for some reason only God knows, I'm the one chosen to endure this battle.

༄ ༄ ༄ ༄ ༄ ༄

Nearly two months have passed since my surgery. Exercising, eating well and feeling great describe my daily routine. Time for me to start back to work. Leaving my students without having a chance to say good-bye was frustrating. One day I was there, and the next... no Mrs. McCormick. Do they feel as if I deserted them? My return to school depends on Dr. Segreti's approval. When I call the office, I am shot down. The nurse reminds me that physical strength is vital for the next phase of this journey. Permission to return to work can't be granted until Dr. Segreti sees me. She tells me to be patient and spend time healing and getting healthy.

My Type A personality is not happy about this. God is teaching me patience. I'm learning to *smell the roses*...and the marigolds, and the tulips, grass, and weeds! Hours are passed sitting on our back patio, swinging back and forth. The birds and the squirrels racing around our yard are great entertainment, but do I have to check out the bugs, too? Can you tell I am quite restless? These long, idle hours are what I used to long for; hours of quiet time to meditate, pray and read. Life used to be so busy. Now my days allow time to play flute and piano, read the Bible and memorize scripture. This is a time when I'm able to grow closer to the Lord. I learn to treasure these days.

∾∾∾∾∾∾

My appointment with Dr. Segreti arrives. She is pleased with my healing. Now it's time to have a PICC line placed in my left arm. The line is placed into one of the large veins above my elbow and then threaded into a large vein above my heart. It doesn't hurt as they insert the catheter. Lying perfectly still, I put myself into a place of peace and prayer during this procedure. For the next six months, two tubes will dangle four inches out of my left arm.

The nurse who transports me back to *short stay* confides to me that she is a one year survivor of breast cancer. We share our stories and she tells me that it's okay to be angry. I say that I'm not angry. I'm just glad it's me and not another member of my family with this disease. Again she tells me not to feel guilty about getting angry now and then. Maybe in the future her advice will be needed. Right now, I still don't realize what lies ahead for us. This nurse also tells me that only cooked or peeled fruits and vegetables are allowed. So much for my everyday snack of red grapes... and no more salad for me. This will be hard, as I may be part rabbit, and salads are my favorite food.

I wait in the short stay area for my turn to have an abdominal port put in. The choice to receive chemo through both an

IV and an abdominal port is easy. Dr. Segreti likes this method. My quality of life will be somewhat more compromised with an abdominal port and IV for chemo, but Rod and I both want whatever offers the greatest percentage for survival. Am I really talking about survival? Rod reminds me that this too is only for a short time. This too shall pass. I know he is right. He is my rock, my cheerleader, and my best friend. *Lord, I thank You for him time and time again. How do people get through this when they have no support system? No hope in You?*

We wait hours for my port surgery. Rod and I are fine, though, because we understand that Dr. Segreti is tied up in surgery with another person who has cancer. It was just two months ago that it was me on the surgical table, holding up others waiting for their minor operations because of complications with mine. No complaining or lack of patience is allowed, as I would much rather be where I am now on this journey, than the person in surgery.

Finally, the surgery is done. Two small additional wounds are on my stomach, as well as more stitches. So much for ever wearing a two piece bathing suit again. Not a big deal. After all, I *am* fifty-one years old. I'm just getting tired of feeling like a Thanksgiving turkey! How many more times will I be cut open before it's all over? There is now a rubber ball with nearly a foot long catheter in my abdomen. It's under the skin and bulges out where it's placed. My sex appeal is getting harder to hang onto with each passing day!

Recovery goes well. Rod plays nurse to me throughout the night, but I'm not really experiencing any problems. In order to shower, he has to wrap my left arm in plastic. My PICC line and my new incision need to stay dry. These directions leave me standing backwards in the shower, praying that the days fly by. It's overwhelming how this never ends. There always seems to be something else to deal with.

ഗ ഗ ഗ ഗ ഗ ഗ

Rod leaves for a job site out of state today. This doesn't worry me because I made it through the night without getting sick. Kaycee offers to come and stay with me, or have me sleep at her house. While her offer is deeply appreciated, Nicolette is home right now and able to take care of any needs that may arise. What a strange feeling it is to have your children caring for you, rather than the other way around. Nicolette and I spend the day at home together watching television and some movies that Hope sent over. Finally, it is night. Time to go back to bed. Unfortunately, the night does not go as well as we hoped. I'm grabbing my cell phone beside my bed and calling Nicolette for help. "Nicolette!"

"What's wrong, Mom?" She is groggy and half asleep.

"I'm sick!" She hears the noises I'm making. Her footsteps hurry quickly into the kitchen as she grabs me a bowl. Lucky for me, there's a trash can nearby. This is awful. How did a six and a half hour surgery not make me nauseous, but a fifteen minute operation does? Nicolette is in my room pulling the trash can aside and shoving the bowl in front of me.

"Mom, what's wrong with you?"

She is not used to me being sick. Mothers are always the caretakers. Let's face it, mothers keep going with sore throats, fevers, and diarrhea. We are not supposed to get ill. We don't have time for all of that. "It's the anesthetic," I tell her. After she is sure that I'm finished and all cleaned up, Nicolette heads back to her room. Feeling much better now, and snuggling under the covers, sleep returns.

Half an hour later, I'm dialing Nicolette's phone again. Once more her help is quickly needed. What did we do before cell phones? Without my phone, Nicolette wouldn't hear me calling for her on the other side of the house. While I'm relieved that she is home, it saddens me that she has to see me like this. She's showing signs of stress from all of her school work, and now my illness is adding to it. Rod will be home by supper time today. This makes me happy because Nicolette's shift needs to be over.

My stomach seems to have settled down. All day long I do nothing more than watch television and read. Rod is back now and drives Nicolette up to school. Perseverance and determination are two qualities a student must have to attend Grove City College. The "Harvard of Western Pennsylvania" is its local nickname. While the academics are rigorous, Nicolette is happy that she finally fits in with the students and the Christian belief system she finds there. I admire her for sticking it out and not giving up. Perhaps she is tougher than me.

✍ ✍ ✍ ✍ ✍ ✍

Nicolette is only back at school for a few days before she calls and asks to be picked up. She was having difficulty taking antibiotics for a sinus infection several months ago. Since then she is experiencing weight loss, a lack of appetite, and more anxiety than is usual for her. Rod and I are concerned and know that she needs medical help. After some initial frustration, blood tests and a lower GI are ordered. Her thyroid counts are excessive and she is anemic. Her weight has dropped from one hundred twenty-three pounds to one hundred five pounds in two short months. She is later diagnosed as suffering from Hashimoto's disease, an autoimmune disorder that affects the thyroid, and is referred to a hematologist. The only positive thing about all of this is that my daughter's health issues take the focus off of me. No one seems to be able to identify what causes a thyroid problem, but I'm convinced stress plays a huge part in it. Her health problems are just too coincidental to the timing of my own illness. Throughout all of this, our family realizes how important a sense of humor is.

Nicolette asks Rod, "Hey, Dad, Kaycee has a gynecologist, Mom has an oncologist, I have an endocrinologist. What do you have?"

Without missing a beat, Rod looks at Nicolette and says, "Just give me two weeks, and I'll need a psychologist!"

He gives all of us a good laugh, and we need that right now.

৵৵৵৵৵৵

Mother's Day arrives. Kaycee, the artist, always creates gifts that hold such meaning. When I read *The 5 Love Languages* by Gary Chapman, I realized that her love language is definitely *Gifts*. Everything she gives involves deep thought into its selection or creation. This makes each present received from Kaycee extremely special. On this day, Kaycee gives me four ceramic birds that she designed. There is a 'father' bird, a 'mother' bird, and two 'children.' The birds rest on our dining room table. It pleases me to know that she took her time, making these birds unique for me.

There are teal colored feathers delicately swirling on the birds. I love them. Weeks later, Nicolette points out just how special the birds are that Kaycee gave me. If you follow the teal paint of the 'mother' bird, the color flows into the ribbon symbol for ovarian cancer awareness. I never noticed this until Nicolette spotted it. Kaycee can be one of the most thoughtful people. I'm so proud of her right now.

✆✆ ✆✆ ✆✆ ✆✆ ✆✆ ✆✆

The time is approaching for me to begin my chemo. I wonder how in the world they are going to put a needle into my stomach where the port lies under the skin. The site of the port is still tender from its insertion during surgery. I'll be awake during all of this. I quickly push these thoughts to the back of my mind. I'm determined to enjoy these few days before the next stage of our journey begins.

Because I'll be at the hospital anywhere from five to eight hours for my treatments, buying a laptop sounds like a good idea to me. I love to read and write, and it may help pass the time while I'm hooked up to the IV. I mention this idea to Mom, and within a day my stepfather has dragged me to Staples with the intent of buying a laptop. It is far too extravagant a gift, but my mother tells me to accept it. Tom feels this is one way he can help.

This demonstration of Tom's love means so much. He suggests I write an article or two. Even if all I do is record my thoughts, the writing will be therapeutic for me. Putting my feelings into words makes me feel better. I will always be grateful for this special present from Tom and Mom.

4

Chemo: Part One

My *Welcome to Chemo* packages are here. We are clearly overwhelmed, wondering what all of it is for, and where we should put everything. I'm about to cry. There are numerous boxes filled with medical supplies like gauze pads, an IV pole, blood draw supplies, and lots more. It makes me sick to my stomach to look at everything, knowing it's all for me.

"What are we supposed to do with all of this?" Frustration is taking over. I want to shove it all into a closet where no one can see it! "These supplies make me feel like a hoarder on that awful television show! We can't even walk through the dining room anymore!"

Rod takes over. He is in control. I can tell Rod has already put himself into the *fix it* mode that men so often take on in times of need. Always, when my emotions are ready to break, he takes control of the situation and makes me feel as though everything is all right.

"It's fine, Kim. I'll get it organized for us. Don't even worry about it." He gets a compartment of drawers out of his office and starts dividing up all of the supplies.

"I really don't want all of this stuff out in the open where everyone can see it, Rod." My pleas sound ridiculous even to myself. We have no room to put these supplies anywhere but out in the open. Where exactly do I expect him to put it all?

Rod comes to me, and strokes my back. "It will be fine, Kim. It's only temporary. Out here in the open, the supplies will be handy for anyone who needs them."

I know he's right, but turning my dining room into a temporary hospital is not my idea of quality home interior design!

Soon we receive a call from my home care nurse. He leaves a message on my answering machine.

"Good morning, Mrs. McCormick. My name is Duane Dicks. I'll be providing you with your home care nursing needs. If you would give me a call soon, we can set up a time for me to talk with you and your family caregivers about your upcoming medical needs... ."

You might think that a call from the nurse would concern me, and while it does, my husband and I cannot help but burst into laughter. I have a nephew named Dwayne. He is quite a character, always involved in some kind of situation that leaves you just shaking your head and asking yourself, how in the world did he get himself into that?!

"I can't believe my nurse is named Dwayne!" I laugh. "How many people are named that?"

We continue to laugh, I guess because we are imagining my nephew being my nurse. My nephew has a *very* caring heart, so if all Dwaynes are like him, I will be in good hands. I do discover later, though, that the two Dwaynes spell their names differently. My nephew is Dwayne, my nurse is Duane. He turns out to be quite a character, too. Thankfully, he also has a kind and caring heart... must be something about the name.

ぺ ぺ ぺ ぺ ぺ ぺ

It's fortunate that I'm not superstitious. If I were, the date of my first chemo treatment would be postponed. The scheduled date is Friday, May 13, 2011.

My friend, Linda, who is a cancer survivor, visits me.

"Tell me honestly, Linda, how's chemo going to be?" My concern is obvious.

She looks me in the eye, smiles, and says, "You'll be all right."

To me, that means, *it's bad, but you'll survive.* I don't like the sound of this, but I don't really have a choice, do I?

Both prior to and after each chemo treatment I am required to take a *cocktail* of prescribed meds (cocktail...hmmm...maybe this is why I don't drink). It's all very confusing, so keeping a list of my medications and the time each is taken in a journal is helpful. Keeping all of this straight is a real challenge. It's hard not to gag on all of the pills. The greatest number I take at one time is nine, but before the day is over, there are numerous more added to the mix.

The first step is to report to Dr. Segreti's office to be weighed, measured, and have my vitals taken. Then onto Kathy Rodicus' room where there are four recliners for patients. Kathy is my chemo nurse. She's very pleasant, encouraging, and assures me that I will do just fine. Rod comes in with me. We're glad that I'm the only patient coming today. This allows Kathy a lot of time to explain what will happen.

My treatment combines three drugs: Cisplatin, Taxotere, and Taxol. I receive the Cisplatin and Taxotere on Day 1, then I go home and return one week later on Day 8 for the Taxol. After my Day 8 chemo, the following week is treatment free. Kathy says that typically patients report the side effects of Day 1 as being worse than Day 8.

"Let's get started," I say. The sooner we get this started, the sooner it will be over with. I choose the recliner directly in front of the television. It is the second one from the door. Rod sits closest to the wall where he can plug in his computer. We're thankful that he has wireless accessibility in this room, as he will spend many hours working from this little nook while I'm receiving my chemo.

Ellen DeGeneres is on the television, so that lightens the mood a little. Watching her dance throughout her audience always makes me laugh; in fact, this usually gets me out of my seat and dancing along with her! Not today, though.

First, Kathy puts some medicine in a bag on the pole to my left. It's quite a cocktail...there's that word again. There is some Benadryl in the mix that makes me drowsy, but something also causes restless leg syndrome; each time I feel myself drifting off, my legs shake and wake me up.

The IV drip is running very slowly this first time. Kathy wants to monitor how my body reacts to the medicines. After nearly four hours, she uses a numbing spray several times on my stomach where the port is.

"Do you want to hold your husband's hand?" Kathy asks me. At first I'm not sure why she is asking me this.

"Of course," I say, "I'd love to hold his hand," but then I see the large needle that she is holding. I realize the needle is meant for me. It will be going directly into my abdomen through the port. Kathy is very good and quickly slips in the syringe. My next round of medicine is being delivered. Kathy packs gauze pads around the needle to keep it secure until my session is over.

It is a long day. The process is finished at six o'clock. Kathy assures us that it only takes this long on our first visit. Since all went well, she'll be able to allow the drip to go faster on future visits. On my way home to New Castle, which is a good hour from West Penn Hospital in Pittsburgh, I am to *swish* or *slosh* the medicines around in my abdomen by flopping back and forth from side to side. I have to switch sides every fifteen minutes. Anti-nausea medicine helps me arrive home without getting sick along the way.

When we're finally home, I relax and check #1 off of my list. Only eleven more times to go. At bedtime I take a sleeping pill. There are also three types of anti-nausea pills on the menu. I'm queasy, but don't vomit. Throughout the night, nausea wakes me several times, but soon after taking the medicines, this goes away.

⟪⟫ ⟪⟫ ⟪⟫ ⟪⟫ ⟪⟫ ⟪⟫

The next day, Luke is graduating from college. He understands that I cannot make the ceremony. This is one of the first important events that chemo causes me to miss. *Lousy* is a polite way to describe how I'm feeling. Or, more like a Mack truck ran me over in my sleep, then backed up on me one more time, just to make sure the job was well done!

For five days, in addition to the anti-nausea meds, I take steroids and stool softeners. My stomach is bloated from all of the chemotherapy drugs going into my abdomen. Looking four months pregnant causes me to delve into my drawers and closets on a search to find any blouse that will disguise this.

My home nurse stops in today. Duane teaches Rod how to hook up my IV fluids. I'll receive these for five days after each Day 1 chemo treatment. Duane has a great disposition and laugh. These are both wonderful qualities to have when visiting ill patients. Our conversations give my day a needed lift.

"You know, Kim," he says, "I respect what you do, being a teacher. That has to be a rewarding job. I always wanted to be one."

Because I enjoy Duane's temperament and competence, I say, "Well, I'm glad you became a nurse instead!" Between Rod and Duane, I will be well taken care of.

The next morning, we attend church. The back row becomes our new seat, since Kathy warned me to be very cautious of picking up illnesses while going through chemo. With a low white blood cell count I will be pretty vulnerable to infections. During the service, nausea and heat consume me. Clearly, I have overdone it. Part of me wants to be the person who is able to fight through this disease, participating in life as if nothing has changed. Unfortunately, a *chemo fatigue* arrives that day, which levels me on the couch.

Three days have passed since the first chemo session and this fatigue, which Dr. Segreti said was to be expected, is beyond my imagining. It's not just being very tired... it is being so completely unable to move that I sit and watch golf and a car race all day long. In my opinion, these are two of *the most* boring sports on TV, and yet I don't have enough energy to pick up the remote control to change the station. I come to understand the meaning of *chemo fatigue.*

Time for another IV bag. After Rod hooks me up, I sleep awhile in the recliner. Being unable to move my bowels since Thursday night makes me quite uncomfortable. Constipation can be a side effect of chemo. Obviously, this is going to be a problem for me.

❧ ❧ ❧ ❧ ❧ ❧

By Monday the constipation is so bad that I'm curled up on our bed. My stomach is hard and tight, the muscles contracted and aching. A phone call to Kathy in Pittsburgh results in trying the *bomb.* It's a mixture of equal parts milk of magnesia and prune juice. All I know is that it gags me to drink it, and it *still* does not work.

By late afternoon, Rod is ready to take me to the emergency room. He calls Kathy again, and this time her advice is that if I don't have luck soon, Rod needs to take me to the ER. I do NOT want to go to the hospital. With all of my regular appointments and treatments, any additional trips to the hospital are verboten.

After a trip to the pharmacy, Rod brings me suppositories. This provides some relief. Lying on the bathroom floor, my dear husband helps me use an enema. This is humiliating for me, but my determination to solve this problem without a hospital prevails. Perhaps Rod should be a nurse. He is so kind and helpful. I'm embarrassed that this type of help is needed, but so thankful my husband is willing to assist me in getting well, no matter what he has to do for me. It's possible to keep loving a person more and more, even when you think you already love them as much as is humanly possible.

Full relief finally comes, and we all celebrate. How ridiculous all of this is! I'm absolutely thrilled because I had a bowel movement! A sense of humor is something that Rod and I promise to maintain. Praying and laughing are the best medicines for this condition, and in that order.

Six days after Day 1 of chemo, normalcy finally returns. But guess what? It's time to go back for Day 8. Day 8 is when I receive Taxol, along with many other meds. This is the one and only time that my personal *chauffeur*, my steadfast husband, Rod, is unable to take me for my treatment. Mom and Tom volunteer for the job. I'm thankful that they are in Pennsylvania and available to help us.

Mom stays with me in the chemo room, while Tom goes to another appointment he has in Pittsburgh. This time I hold Mom's hand while the needle is pushed into my stomach. Kathy is always very conscientious about my comfort. She knows her job well and makes the insertion quickly.

Treatment only takes about six hours. Steroids and anti-nausea meds are on the menu, but after Day 8 there are no IV fluids. Arriving home, I check another one off. Only ten more chemo treatments to go.

Five days later things turn around. This morning an amazing feeling has returned – normalcy! Shaking Rod in bed, I tell him, "I think I will be okay today! I think I feel normal!" What a great feeling!

Dr. Segreti does not have a problem with me returning to work when I'm feeling up to it, but she cautions me to be careful when my white blood cell counts drop. Just being back to work helps me feel alive and productive. Turn that television set off. I've watched more television in the past two and a half months than I did in the past year.

ᔓ ᔓ ᔓ ᔓ ᔓ ᔓ

My church is like comfort food to me, I can't get enough of it. A special peace washes over me, as soon as I sit down in the pew. During this peaceful time, the problems of the outside world are blocked out. As long as my health allows, I will continue to attend church every week.

ᔓ ᔓ ᔓ ᔓ ᔓ ᔓ

Twelve days have passed since my first chemo treatment. When showering, I realize that there is no hair on my legs anymore. No stubs, just nice smooth legs. Ahhhh, the irony of it all, like winning a free cruise when you suffer with unremitting sea sickness. Not having to shave my legs for a while is a bonus, but it is also foreshadowing what is to come.

My nose also begins to run furiously. At first, my thought is that I'm catching a cold, but then I realize something –no nose hairs. Most of the time we think that nose hair is gross, but now I realize why it's so important.

Then one morning, while washing my hair, a large clump of blonde sticks to my fingers. Ignoring the first strands, I try to rinse the shampoo ever so gently. There's no denying that my scalp is tender and giving up its beautifully thick hair. I pray that I might be one of those individuals who do not lose *all* of their hair. Yes, they lose some, but not enough that they have to wear a wig.

For a couple of days, my hair loss doesn't faze me too much. I am in denial. I cling to the hope that I have plenty of hair. Mom offers to buy me a wig—when and if it is necessary. My first thought is that I'll just buy cute hats, but when my hair continues to fall out, I call Mom and say, "It's time, Mom. I think you need to call about a wig."

We set up an after-hours appointment at Rebecca's Salon. The salon is in an older home in New Wilmington that has been renovated into a welcoming haven for weary women in need of some pampering. The interior, where plenty of polished wood surrounds you, offers a homey experience. No one else is at the salon, as Becky realizes what a difficult appointment this is for me.

Selling wigs is not typically a part of Becky's business, but for clients with medical conditions, she is willing to offer her expertise in helping us obtain one. Kaycee and Mom come with me for my wig choosing appointment. There are several styles available for me to try on. I plop a shoulder length wig on my head.

"There. What do you think about this?" Not really wanting to be here, I'm trying to be a good sport and go through the motions with an appreciative attitude.

"If you want a *different* look, it could work." Kaycee's face says it all. I've been around this girl for twenty-plus years, this wig *won't* work—definitely sleek and beautiful, but not me.

"Okay, what about this one?" Trying on a shorter pixie style wig, both Kaycee and Mom's faces light up.

"I like it!" exclaims Kaycee. "That's cute, Mom!"

"Oh, honey, it really looks like you." Mom is smiling, with tears in her eyes.

Seeing this, my eyes well up, too. And then Kaycee is wiping her tears. This scene is like something out of *Tears of Endearment*. Facing the reality of cancer is really starting to hit home. Someone please wake me up and tell me this is all a dream.

Becky lightens the mood with her bubbly personality and her own, "I love it!"

Wanting to show Mom how thankful I am that she's willing to make this purchase for me, I shrug my shoulders and give the small group a smile. "Yea, it *is* cute."

"The color is great, Mom," says Kaycee, "and seriously, if I didn't *know* it was a wig, I *wouldn't* know."

With Kaycee and Mom encouraging me, my wig selection is decided quickly.

My mom is cautious with her money. Raising children on a limited income makes one quite frugal. However, when it comes to choosing a wig for me, she makes sure that it's top of the line, one of the best wigs available.

Rod says he really likes the style. He tells me, "Don't take this wrong, but I might even like it better than how you wear your hair now."

I just smile and say, "Well, that's good, because I think I'll be wearing this for a while."

My hats arrive. I still have some hair left, and I am not jumping to wear the wig. The American Cancer Society carries some very unique styles. I love them. They are easy to throw on each morning. The students at school say "oooh" and "awww" when they see the hats. One fourth grader even tells me I look like a middle schooler with my JLo (Jennifer Lopez) hat on. Now that's a compliment!

✑ ✑ ✑ ✑ ✑ ✑

Each morning I wake up and find my pillow covered with hair. It's getting thinner and thinner. My friend, Linda, offers to shave my head. When she went through cancer, it was easier for her to just get the hair loss over with. Rhonda suggests the same thing. I thank them both for their thoughts, but I'm not ready to shave my head. There's still hope that my hair will hang in there.

One evening when Nicolette is home from school, I begin combing my hair in the bathroom. She is with me, watching. With each stroke the comb fills with clumps of blonde hair. I will be bald.

My tears rise from somewhere deep inside me, from somewhere that I've buried them for months. I cannot control it. The gut wrenching sobs begin, and I cannot stop.

This disease called cancer is finally real to me. For months, denial helped me to keep it together. From the outside, no one could see that anything was wrong with me, but now everyone will know. No matter where I am, I'll be the person with cancer.

Overwhelmed with sadness, I break my own rule; I feel sorry for myself. Leaning against the bathroom sink, I sob. Then I notice that Nicolette is crying next to me. I want to scream at the heavens, "Why?! Why me?! Why us?!

Nicolette and I hang onto each other, crying together for some time. Embracing my child, we eventually calm down. God provides us with a sovereign peace.

"Don't worry," I say. "I'm okay. I guess I just needed a cry. It's healthy every now and then, you know?" I tilt her chin up and kiss her forehead. "It's not a big deal, really. It's just hair, right? It will grow back."

Nicolette is still teary, and tells me it's okay for me to cry, that she would cry, too. Tears allowed my emotions to flow, but now a tremendous headache is left behind in their place. Tackling the problem at hand seems to be a better choice for me now. My anguish is replaced with my resolve to face this situation head on.

Truly, I am blessed, much better off than many people. I cheer Nicolette and myself up by trying on my trendy hats. "Think positively, Nicolette! There's still hair that shows around the brim of my hats! If people just glance at me, they'll never notice that I'm going bald!"

Kaycee arrives for a visit. When she sees my head, she cries, too. "I'm sorry you're losing your hair," she sniffs. Tears are streaming down her face now. This time I'm okay.

"I'll be fine, Kaycee. Earlier, I broke down with your sister, but I think I cried all the tears out of my system!"

Kaycee hugs me. "That's okay, Mom. You're allowed to cry. You *know* how I would be, if this was me."

"I have to make the best of this. It's not like I'm the first, nor the last woman to lose her hair due to chemotherapy."

Kaycee feels better when I remind her that my hair will eventually grow back. All the women of the house have mourned the loss of my hair now. Good. It is done. Let us move on.

∽∽ ∽∽ ∽∽ ∽∽ ∽∽ ∽∽

Nicolette is my designated wig stylist; she comes home from college, and will stay up until midnight when my ready-to-wear hair is in desperate need of a freshening up. But our initial foray into styling was not without its glitches. The wig is styled with a small flip all the way around its ends. Getting this style to look right takes a little practice, but she works on it while it is on the mannequin head. One evening, after Nicolette proclaims my hair is ready to wear, I take the wig from the model and place it on my head. I look like the Flying Nun ready for takeoff. All I need is to catch just the right head wind and I will be airborne. We laugh until the tears are rolling down our cheeks. Words of advice: If you have the time, have your designated stylist, style your wig while wearing it on your *own* head—proportions are everything!

∽∽ ∽∽ ∽∽ ∽∽ ∽∽ ∽∽

I need to briefly share an intimate moment that anyone too close to me may choose not to read, especially if you are my child!

After my surgery, Rod and I find our relationship in the bedroom to be quite altered. Remember, I am now missing all of my inner female parts and then some. Everything I discovered about making love with my husband over the past thirty-two years seems to have changed. Maybe it's because of my mental state right now, or maybe because I'm missing parts that aid in sexual fulfillment. All I know is that while I'm feeling half a woman and maimed, Rod is patient and loving.

I fear that things may never be the same. I know that things are not the same. But will we adjust? The wounds on my body are still tender and sensitive, holding me back from showing Rod the love I feel inside. Nerve endings don't seem to be complete. Will the sensations my body once felt at his touch ever be restored? These questions stick in my mind, playing over and over again, making me long for my younger, healthier body.

Eventually, through much patience on Rod's part, we learn how to compensate for the changes in my body. And literally, the old saying that, "Time heals all wounds," plays out true for us.

The moments following our first evening of fulfilled and satisfied intimacy, is a time of wonder for me. I am lying on the bed with a foot long, bright red scar down my stomach, two other two inch scars on my abdomen, a PICC line with two tubes hanging four inches out of my arm, and a bulging port bumping up out of my abdomen. My fringe of bleach blonde hair circles my head while the bald center shines through in the middle. I try to fathom how my husband finds me even remotely sexually attractive.

I cannot help it. This is my second big cry. These tears are cries of relief, joy, appreciation, thankfulness, and loving passion all at one time pouring out of my soul. My meltdown is not one of sorrow, but tremendous, undying gratitude. This man that God blessed me with has walked next to me these past months every step of the way. How can this man still think I'm beautiful?

Looking at my naked body, I feel like a science experiment. When I look into the mirror I don't even know who the person is looking back. I speak, and it's my voice coming out of that woman. But is that really me?

It is at this time my husband rolls over to look down upon me, smiles and whispers into my ear, "You are beautiful."

Rod doesn't care, he loves me. His loving arms wrap around me and hold me close. This is truly a Godly love. There is no other explanation for it. I am blessed beyond measure.

✍ ✍ ✍ ✍ ✍ ✍

School is now out. I managed six days of work before summer arrived. It is good that summer is here. I'll be able to have time off without using up all of my sick days. Sessions 3 and 4 of chemo now loom on my schedule. While I'm there I meet another lady suffering with cancer. It is obvious that she has lots of experience at this chemo thing. She's very kind and encouraging to me.

As Kathy is connecting me up to the IV bags of medicine and giving me my pills, I overhear this woman telling her friend that she ate some cottage cheese the other day, and just how delicious it tasted. She said, "I don't know what it was about it, maybe the texture, or its creaminess, but it was one of the best things I've eaten in a long time."

When I hear these words, I wonder if my sense of taste is going to be affected by the chemo. A metallic taste in the mouth is a common side effect of chemo patients after treatment.

Luckily, the day is over in about six hours. Now that Kathy knows I'm able to tolerate the medicines, she runs the medicines faster. The only time Rod leaves my side is to run down to the cafeteria for his lunch. Even then, he brings it back up to the chemo room to sit next to me while we eat together. I don't really have an appetite, but I eat to keep up my strength.

Everywhere I go in the hospital, people comment on the cuff I wear over my PICC line. Kaycee, always the artist, made me numerous adorable cuffs out of stretchy cloth to put over the PICC line tubes so that they are snug up against my arm. She supplied me with every color I need, so that my cuff matches my clothing. If she wanted to, she could start a business of making these and be very successful. She adds some shiny bling to the cuffs so that I sparkle!

On our way home I recline in my seat and slosh back and forth, as directed. My nausea may be from the chemo or car sickness; all I know is that I'm miserable and bloated. Determined to *not* experience constipation again, I took a stool softener last night and will take one every night for months to come. Unfortunately, I will also have to use suppositories for months to come. It's pretty sad when the topic of your conversations is whether or not you feel nauseated and if you have had a bowel movement. What's that saying about the small things in life bringing us our greatest joys?

I allow myself to take a prescribed sleeping pill the night before chemo and the night of my chemo. But that's it. No more than those two pills. I don't want to become addicted to any medicines.

Tonight, despite waking up briefly with nausea several times, I fall into a deep sleep. I'm dreaming, and in my dream I'm growing wet. A dry place is all I'm looking for, but I just keep getting wetter and wetter. You know where this is going, right? Low and behold, I have wet the bed. My poor husband... not only has he had to help me with an enema, but now he is making his way to the laundry room with a pile of crumpled sheets and mattress pad in the middle of the night. Despite the desperation of our circumstances, we find humor. Rod's eyes twinkle and he smiles. "Do I need to put a diaper on you?"

I burst out laughing. I thank him for his help in cleaning up the bed, and then I apologize and thank him again. I'm crying, I am laughing. This is what life has become. Rod just shakes his head and chuckles under his breath. *Thank you, Jesus, for a man with a sense of humor. Help me to keep mine.*

✎ ✎ ✎ ✎ ✎ ✎

We are blessed that Rod's sister, Tammy, is a nurse. Rod has to travel out of town one night, so she's able to come and run my IV for me. Another time, she flushes out my PICC lines on her lunch break. I hate asking people for their help, but Rod's sister makes it easy for me to ask. Every family needs at least one nurse.

✎ ✎ ✎ ✎ ✎ ✎

It is not long before I realize just how much my sense of taste is affected by chemo. Interestingly, things like peppermint gum or wintergreen mints, which I love, are quite distasteful to me. Normally, I drink water all day long. Now water makes me want to gag. Just to get my medicine down is a chore. The only type of meat I care to eat is hamburger in any fashion—meatballs, meat loaf, and burgers. This is so strange, because I'm a chicken and fish lover. Rarely do I eat red meat.

My sisters have friends who have experienced chemo, and they recommend foods I may like. Rhonda and Jamie show up with rice, Jell-O, fruit cups, Starburst candy, Pedialyte freeze pops and much more. How sweet are my sisters? Very. Often they will come and keep me company when I don't know what to do with myself. Even having one of my sisters just sitting on the couch next to me gives me comfort. They also drive Dad out to visit me from time to time when I'm having a good day. It is healthy for him to get out for a visit, and it's healthy for me to see him. I miss him.

Time for another round of chemo. For the next twelve days I will not feel well. First are my five days with IV fluids at home. The bloating will last for at least four days. My face will appear sunburned; they call this a *moon face*, when it's round and puffy from the steroids. Typically, my throat will be quite sore for a few days. On day 7, I will begin to feel a little better, perhaps even get out to the grocery store. On Day 8, it is back to Pittsburgh for chemo, and I will be down again. After five days, I will feel well. I know the good days are coming when water, once again, tastes delicious. All of the foods I used to enjoy become tasty once again. I will treasure the following two weeks. These are the days when I feel perfectly healthy. It's hard to believe I'm sick, but all too soon it's time to go back to Pittsburgh and start the cycle all over again.

Now that I know how this goes, I suppose it's easier. At least, I can make plans for fun things to do on my good days. My niece is getting married in June. It will be wonderful to get together with all my family. God is good. My niece's wedding actually falls on a weekend when I should feel well. This gives me something to look forward to.

Nicolette and I go shopping for new dresses. I want to scream for joy just because I feel well enough to get in the car and drive to Sears. Ordinary, everyday life experiences are like dessert to me. I don't have them often, but savor every morsel when given the chance. God has given me so much to treasure and appreciate. But now, when my own mortality confronts me daily, every breath I breathe is sweeter.

✍ ✍ ✍ ✍ ✍ ✍

Co-workers at school are certainly *paying it forward* in honor of me. How blessed I am to have such caring people surrounding me.

Ali holds a jewelry party, with Kaycee as the saleslady. As hostess, Ali earns over three hundred dollars in free jewelry. Instead of selecting jewelry for herself, she passes the earnings over to me and provides me with a fantastic shopping experience from home. Ali stops over every Tuesday morning with her little girl. I frequently tell her how much her visits mean to me, but I'm sure she cannot truly comprehend how deeply I mean this. Sometimes I think I look like *walking death*, but since Ali is like my third daughter, she's allowed to see me this way. Ali's little girl is so young that she just loves me no matter what. We can learn so much from toddlers. They don't care what a person looks like; they just love you for who you are.

Recently, Kaycee started giving away teal-colored bracelets symbolizing ovarian cancer awareness as door prizes at her jewelry parties.

Another co-worker, Kathy, runs a 5K race in my honor. She mails me a great card with her picture showing her race #669 attached to her teal-colored T-shirt representing ovarian cancer. What an inspiration she is.

A third grade teacher, Diane, holds a fund raiser for cancer research selling make-up to the staff of Wilmington schools. Lucky me, she gives me a new compact with lipstick and blush inside.

My mentor teacher, Tike (it's her nickname), from the first year I began teaching school, calls every week to check up on me. She can tell from my voice if I'm doing well or not. When I am well, we talk for quite a while. When I'm not well, she makes her call short and sweet, and says, "You don't feel well, do you, honey? I won't keep you. I just want you to know I'm thinking about you." But even that short call means the world to me.

My Aunt Barb stops by with a hand-made prayer shawl. The note attached reads: As you wear this shawl may you be cradled in hope, kept in joy, graced with peace and wrapped in love! Family and friends, priceless.

I try to imagine going through this experience alone. What does a person do who is not surrounded by a phenomenal family and group of friends? More importantly, how does a person survive an experience such as this without faith in God? He gives me hope. He gives me strength. He gives me reassurance that all is well and that He is in control of my life. I pray for the people who are alone and suffering. Perhaps my prayers will send these unknown people comfort.

∽ ∽ ∽ ∽ ∽ ∽

Nicolette asks me if I will sing with her one Sunday at Luke's church, Castlewood Christian and Missionary Alliance. This is where Luke's father, Rev. Jim O'Hara, is a minister. I always feel so welcome and accepted when we visit there. Rod and I appreciate the love and encouragement the congregation gives Nicolette. We look at my calendar and pick a Sunday that should be a *feel good* day. Next, I select a song, "How You Live" (by Cindy Morgan) with a special message, one that shares a little of my testimony. The lyrics touch your soul. "How You Live" reminds us to embrace each moment and to live each day in a way that is pleasing to our God. It teaches us that life is about serving others, not ourselves. A life lived selfishly returns little joy. It's not how much money we have or how important our positions may be that make life matter. As young children, our parents teach us that it is better to give than to receive. When the magic of those words is finally understood and practiced, that's when our lives shine forth with God's love. That is when we make a difference.

Numerous family members surprise me and show up at Castlewood to support Nicolette and me that Sunday. Mom, Tom, my sisters, and my nephews are there. A lot of tears are shed that morning. God uses our situations to enrich other people's lives if we allow Him to do so.

❧ ❧ ❧ ❧ ❧ ❧

Kaycee is finally feeling well. She looks absolutely adorable with her baby bump. I'm so proud of my daughter. She will make a wonderful mother. Kaycee and her husband, Tim, have already rescued two cats. If they care for their baby even half as much as they spoil those cats, he will be a very lucky little boy. At the end of this journey, my grandson will be arriving. Now *that* is inspiration. One day I'll tell this baby how much he inspired his Nana Kim during her year of illness to keep fighting the fight.

❧ ❧ ❧ ❧ ❧ ❧

Nurse Duane stops in on Tuesday mornings to change the dressings on my PICC line and to draw blood. He has the perfect personality for a home care nurse. Those who knew him in high school ask me, "Are you sure we are talking about the same Duane?" They tell me he was a crazy character during his youth. I assure them that Duane is handling my care quite competently. He is one of many new friends I make during my illness. His smile and upbeat attitude always lift my spirits. Rod calls him Doc Hollywood. Duane tells me I look great in hats. When you have no hair, his compliment means that much more.

My hats fulfill my fashion longings. The newsboy styles are my favorites. I consider wearing one of my hats to my niece's wedding, but opt for my wig instead. Sometimes you just want to blend in with the crowd. My wig helps me to do this.

❧ ❧ ❧ ❧ ❧ ❧

Time to celebrate! My niece, Lisa, is getting married and I'm tired of being sick. With my new dress and wig on, I'm ready to party (at least as much is possible). My wig is not comfortable to me yet, since I wear my hats all of the time, but I'm excited to feel well and to be going to such a happy occasion.

The wedding is awesome. Lisa and her fiancé get married at First Baptist Church. This is the church I've attended since age thirteen, and Rod has attended since birth. We met here, and we married here. It's almost like a second home to us. While I watch the young couple share their vows, all the details of my own wedding in this peaceful sanctuary come back to me. Rod and I stood on the very same spot where they stand now. I remember everything right down to the light blue tuxes. The entire ceremony takes me back to 1979 when Rod and I stood before God and our loved ones, promising Him that we would stay committed to each other throughout our lives. Times like this almost make you feel thirty years younger. All they need to do is play "You Light Up My Life," by Debby Boone and I'll be transported back to that day.

Would I really want to go back to being nineteen years old again, though? The wisdom that all of these years bring is golden. Never would I trade my wisdom for youth. Well, okay, maybe on those days when the tendonitis in my knee and the neuroma in my foot are acting up, I would make a trade. But honestly, the love Rod and I shared when we married has multiplied beyond any of my young bride dreams. The kind of love we share now takes years of happiness and heartache to mature. I don't want to go back, but

I'm prayerfully thankful for the years of memories we have and for the years of memories we continue to make.

On the way to the reception, we stop at my mom and Tom's farm. It's such a beautiful place to take some pictures. These will be keepsakes for years to come. I think of the time my stepsister, Amy, was married here at the farm. We took a picture of Nicolette on their small bridge over the creek, standing there in her flower girl dress, ringlets in her hair and a smile filled with baby teeth. It's one of my all-time favorite pictures of Nicolette as a little girl. Today Nicolette laughs as I make her go over to the same spot on the bridge where she stood as a flower girl fifteen years ago. She poses for a picture standing in the same profile, hands on the bridge rail looking over her shoulder toward the camera. Click. Perfect.

My dad is with us for the evening. He's being a real trooper. Though still in mourning for Helen, he has joined us and is trying to enjoy this day. At the reception, all of the family is there. Of course, everyone wants to know how I'm doing. Just being out among people is a great lift for my spirit.

Rod and I dance only one slow song. This is not like us. We LOVE to dance together. One of our greatest awards was winning the disco dance contest at my senior prom, the night we became engaged. Rod looked so handsome in his light yellow suit with his jet black hair. Our prize was an album of the *Saturday Night Fever* soundtrack. We walked away from that one with our heads held high!

But tonight there will be only one slow dance for us. In his arms, I lay my head on his shoulder and thank God for giving us this day of health. We relax and watch the others have fun. This is okay with me. It's wonderful to be out of the house.

My chemo nurse, Kathy, warns me about being around so many people. My white blood cell counts get dangerously low, and if I get sick, that will put my chemo way behind schedule. On the other hand, I can't stand to "live like I'm dying," as the great country song goes. I understand what Tim McGraw meant in those lyrics, but I want to live as if I am going to live!

⚖ ⚖ ⚖ ⚖ ⚖ ⚖

It's been many years since I figured out that happiness derives from all of the normal moments in life. Reading *I love you*, on a card that Kaycee gives me; watching Tim take care of her as she expects their first child; seeing the way Nicolette and Luke look at each other; feeling Rod next to me in bed and snuggling up against his warm body (until I have a hot flash, of course); eating dinner together. If death comes tomorrow, I will have had one of the most charmed lives a person could enjoy.

⚖ ⚖ ⚖ ⚖ ⚖ ⚖

The week after my niece's wedding it's time to go back for the start of another round of chemo. I dread Day 1. They make me feel like I'm being poisoned. At some point in my treatment all of the following drugs are put into my system: Cisplatin, Taxotere, Taxol, Decadron, Benadryl, Lasix, Ativan, Ondansetron, Promethazine, Neulasta, Neupogen, Anzemet, Mannitol, Aloxi, Zantac, magnesium oxide, potassium, and Tylenol.

I understand that everyone is trying to save my life, but I feel like they are trying to kill me first. There are times I wonder if I'm dying. I keep going, trying not to voice my negative thoughts. Rod is always so positive; I can't let him hear me doubt my survival.

Only *once* do I allow myself to think that perhaps it would be best if I died. I'm feeling so sick. I can't do anything for myself. I think perhaps it would be better to close my eyes, go to sleep, and not wake up. Heaven, and all of the mystery beyond will be revealed to me. That will be awesome! My family will be sad for a time, but eventually, life will go on, and they will not need to worry about me.

Becoming a burden on my family, especially Rod, is a deep concern of mine. I wonder what kind of life he has, always taking care of me. He chooses to stay home with me any time he's invited to go places. He's canceled several flights when scheduled to go to sites for work. He never says it's because of me, but I know that he worries when I'm not feeling well. Always the protector, he stays close by.

I don't want Rod's life to be only about taking care of me. There are times when all I want to do is look at him. While he sleeps I memorize the lines around his eyes and the crook in his nose where he broke it twice. His black hair is beginning to fade into gray. He's earned every one of those gray hairs. Raising two daughters and caring for a sick wife is enough stress to turn any color hair to gray.

Taking in everything about him, I study his handsome face, his dark skin, the strength he shows when he's caring for my PICC lines and wrapping them up for me to shower. I thank him all the time and constantly tell him I couldn't do this without him. Sounding like a schoolgirl in love, I so desperately want Rod to understand my gratitude for all he does. God blessed me with a man who is doing everything he can to make me well and whole again.

> *This one time when death seems more practical than life, I look at Rod and pray to myself, Lord, are you ready to take me home, because what life is now does not seem like life to me. The following verse gives me peace: For me to live is Christ, and to die is gain.*
>
> *Philippians 1:21(NIV)*

God gently speaks to us in times like these, if we are open to hearing Him. Despite the fatigue, the constipation and diarrhea, the nausea and everything else that takes my quality of life away, I know it is temporary. As sick as I am, something deep within my innermost being reminds me that God has much for me to do still on this earth. I will be well again. I firmly believe God reveals these truths to me. They give me the strength and perseverance I need. This renewed sense of fighting spirit lifts me up again. With no complaint, I will continue this battle.

৵ ৵ ৵ ৵ ৵ ৵

> *A time to weep and a time to laugh.*
>
> *Ecclesiastes 3:4*

This is a great scripture! When things are not going well, there is nothing better than a good laugh to brighten our day. Despite the difficult times, we find many occasions to laugh.

Nicolette is well known for borrowing my things, which I never see again. One day she asks, "Mom, can I borrow your hairspray?"

With a twinge of frustration, I reply, "I guess so, Nicolette, but would you *please* let me know when you are running out? Then I can buy you more before yours is all gone. I *need* mine, and I can't have you borrowing it all of the time."

She gives me a strange look, but all she says is, "Yea, that's fine, I will."

Suddenly it dawns on me... I don't have any hair! Of course, she can use my hair spray; she can *have* it for goodness sakes. I bust up laughing when I realize how ridiculous I must sound.

I share this revelation with Nicolette. She smiles and says, "I was thinking that same thing, Mom, but I didn't want to say anything."

Sweet girl.

One afternoon I can't find my glasses anywhere. Rod and I look all over the house for them. When was the last time I wore them? We check the bathrooms, the bedroom night stand, by the piano, and even down in the basement where I exercise. Suddenly, out of the corner of my eye, I spot something reflecting light. Looking to my left, I spot my wig on the kitchen counter with a pair of glasses sitting on top of it. Now I remember. I had a hot flash, pulled that wig off of my head, and threw it down on the counter—the glasses must have been on top of my head, both Rod and I laugh.

There is even humor found in the way I'm feeling right now. Mom stops in to check on me and asks, "How are you doing today?"

Quite good-naturedly I answer, "I am having a really good day today. Although, I do have a bad headache, and my stomach really hurts, and I'm constipated again. Other than that I feel really great!"

Mom gives me a questioning look. It dawns on me that what I just said is very contradictory. Her look tells me that she is wondering whether or not I'm being sarcastic with her. The truth is, after what I go through some days, having a bad headache, a stomachache and constipation equals a great day. I sincerely mean that. We laugh, realizing how cancer makes the everyday challenges of life seem small.

New cellulite seems to appear on my thighs overnight. I read somewhere that chemo makes your fat cells larger. I'll take that excuse. It could be the result of instant menopause. I exercise as much as possible and eat right, but gravity always wins. Thank God for small boobs, or they would be down to my waistline right now!

Believing in the philosophy that things can always be worse helps me keep smiling, even when my physical body is changing before my eyes. I have much to be thankful for.

Celebrating my last day of chemo.

Rod and I enjoying my niece's wedding-Yes, that's my wig!

Luke and Nicolette,
they are engaged!

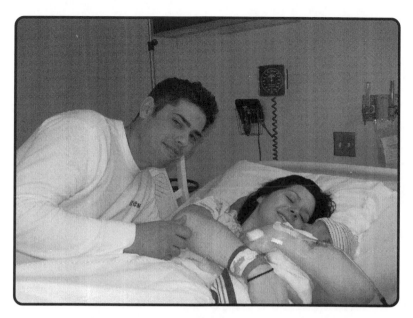

Oct. 3, 2011 Tim, Kaycee and baby Trenton Patrick Aubel.

First day back to school with no wig!

Relay for Life Survivor-Caregiver Walk.

Nana Kim laughing with Trenton.

Tim,Kaycee and Trenton
going to a party!

June 22, 2012 The new Mr. and Mrs. Luke O'Hara.

Kathy Rodicus, my caring chemo nurse.

My home health care nurse Duane, *Doc Hollywood*, Dicks.

One of my angels, Dr. Rifaat Bassaly.

Dr. Eileen Segreti, *the little Italian angel*, as Rod so fondly nick-named her!

5

Chemo: Part Two

Up until this point, my body has bounced back with no problem. When my blood work comes back this week, though, I receive the news that my white blood cell count is too low for me to return for my Day 8 chemo session. My magnesium levels are also too low. Kathy tells me to start taking six magnesium pills a day. Hmmm, there's only one problem with this... I'm running to the bathroom practically every ten minutes.

I call the office in Pittsburgh. This is the only time I whine to them. "You know, I'm trying so hard to be positive and to never complain, but I'm stuck at home all summer in the house. The only activity I can enjoy after chemo is sitting on the swing on our outside patio for days. Now, with all of this magnesium, I can't even do this! I'm running in and out of the house every ten to fifteen minutes. Can you help?"

The nurse talks with Dr. Segreti about my call and gets back to me. They decide to change the magnesium pills to a liquid that will give me the extra magnesium I need through my PICC line. For some reason, when it's delivered directly into my blood stream, my body is able to handle the dosage. This means being connected for two hours a day for three days to the IV pole, though. However, I find this to be the lesser of the two evils.

Learning that my chemo is going to be delayed really gets me down. The remainder of my summer is planned around my chemo appointments. This news is going to throw everything off schedule.

Another week goes by and once again, my white blood cell counts are too low to return for my Day 8 session. The doctor orders a medicine called Neupogen, which I self-administer by injection for the next five days.

Now when they take my blood, my white blood cell count is acceptable, but my potassium is too low for chemo. Come on! What's with the potassium? It has never been a problem! Potassium pills are added to my daily menu. These bring my potassium levels up, but by the time these levels are where they need to be, my white blood cell counts are down again. *Discouraged* is the only word I can think of to describe how I am feeling.

A friend visits and tells me about a young child who is fighting bone cancer. When the little girl has chemo, she has to stay in the hospital for three to four days at a time. She recently lost her leg to the cancer, and they pray she will now be well. At this point, they're not sure.

I cry. Not for myself, but for this beautiful child and her family. *Why, Lord, does a child have to go through cancer? I know we are not to question, but is it really necessary for this little girl and her family to suffer so? Whose life is this tragedy touching for You, Lord? There must be someone who will be saved through this child's illness. Why else would this happen?*

I voice my thoughts, and my friend shares more. The little girl caught her mother crying once. She laid her head on her mother's shoulder and smiled. "Mommy, don't cry because I'm sick," she said. "If I die, I'll get to go to heaven and see Jesus!"

From the mouths of babes, truth is spoken. My down day is over. I'm getting well. The day is near when I will be healed, despite it being a slow, arduous process. Somehow I have to make a difference for others from my experience. *Please show me how I can do this, Lord.*

By the next week, I'm able to return to complete my Day 8 session. Instead of the session being eight days after my Day 1, it's twenty-two days after. I'm upset. Kaycee's baby shower was planned around my chemo, and the way things fall at this time, I won't be able to go to my own daughter's baby shower. The invitations are already mailed, so changing the date is not possible.

Now it's my time to be angry at this disease for all of the trouble it's causing our family. I call Mom, and of course she feels badly. However, within minutes of hanging up, Mom is calling me back with an idea.

"Look, honey, if your next scheduled chemo is going to make you sick for Kaycee's baby shower, why don't you just ask if you can postpone the session until the following week? That way, you will be feeling well when it's time for her shower."

Leave it to a mother to find a solution.

But after this recent setback, I want to catch up on my chemo schedule, not set myself back even further. However, this is my first grandchild being honored, and my daughter's first baby, there is no way this disease is going to keep me from that celebration. Chemo has already caused me to miss Luke's graduation, Nicolette's baptism, and the funeral for Ali's grandfather. I will not let this cancer take Kaycee's baby shower away from me, too.

Dr. Segreti understands the importance of this day for me. I'm sure she knows the mental boost a day like this will give me, too, so my next chemo is postponed until the Tuesday after Kaycee's baby shower.

The most important thing I am forgetting, is leaving God in control. I'm worrying about things I can't change. The only way to find peace at this time is to send my worries upward. The fact is, my body is doing a wonderful job, and I cherish it. How can I become angry with myself for not healing fast enough? My body is trying its very best. From the beginning, Kathy told me there would be setbacks. My belief was that I was strong enough for it to not happen to me. (Sort of the same way I believed I was not going to lose my hair, and we all know how that turned out.)

◌ ◌ ◌ ◌ ◌ ◌

The family pulls together to make Kaycee's baby shower a very special day for all of us. Ali and Nicolette are the hostesses. They spend hours making favors, readying invitations and mailing them, finding prize giveaways and more. Rod and my in-laws prepare the food. He has fruit in a lime sauce, a banana French toast dish, an egg, bacon and cheese casserole and more. No one will go hungry. Kaycee's mother-in-law, Heidi, arrives with gourmet style muffins displayed on tiered glass plates.

This gathering lifts my spirits; well worth the delay of chemo. It's definitely a time that I needed to have. I love seeing everyone; friends from work, family members I have not seen for months, Kaycee's friends and co-workers. Sonogram images of baby Trenton are hanging on the walls in the church basement. God's miracle is right before our eyes. We feel like Trenton is already one of us. The 3-D pictures taken nowadays vividly show his features. I see both Tim and Kaycee in his face. He's a little miracle. I can't wait to be a grandmother.

The celebration renews my determination, I'm encouraged. Everyone tells me how they pray for me every day, and I tell them I feel their prayers. Only four more chemos to go. I can do this. We can do this. Let's get this over with!

∾ ∾ ∾ ∾ ∾ ∾

Anita and Marjorie, who are making this cancer journey as well, arrange for the three of us to meet for brunch. We are all at a point that we feel healthy. It's so important to have a support group. The three of us enjoy talking and sharing because we have all experienced similar trials. I'm able to ask them questions, and vice versa. We help each other. Marjorie tells us that she noticed her eyelashes are filling in. She has more than five or six to enhance with mascara! We congratulate her on this exciting news.

Despite my own hair loss, I still have a slight fringe of hair, as well as my eyebrows and eyelashes. Little do I know that within weeks, all of my eyelashes and eyebrows will be gone, too. An eerie feeling comes over me as I visit with my friends. We're sitting at a four seat table. The three of us from the elementary school have come together to form a sisterhood, so to speak, because of our cancers. The empty seat at our table makes me think, who is next?

∽ ∽ ∽ ∽ ∽ ∽

Rod and I make our next trip to Pittsburgh. It seems like any other day. My first stop is always at Dr. Segreti's office to be weighed and have my vitals taken. When the nurse is certain that these things are fine, we walk across the hall to the chemo room.

We greet Kathy and I settle myself in on my favorite recliner. It's funny how much we are creatures of habit. There are four recliners in the room, and every session I go to the same exact chair, as if it belongs to me. If I arrived and someone else was seated in *my* chair, I don't think I'd be very happy. That never happens, though.

The last few sessions I opt for medicine that helps me to sleep through most of my chemo. *Ellen* entertains me for that first hour, and Rod sits in his corner with his computer working away. At lunch time I wake up and eat something small with Rod before Kathy hooks me up again to start the afternoon's dose of meds.

I'm in a sound sleep when I hear Kathy shaking me, calling my name. "Kim! Kim! Wake up, there's been an earthquake!"

Am I dreaming? An earthquake? This chemo is really playing with my mind.

Again I hear Kathy. "Kim, wake up! There was an earthquake! We may have to evacuate everyone! Are you awake?"

Wow, this really is real! I live in Pennsylvania, for goodness sakes! We're not supposed to get earthquakes here. Rod is by my side as we await the hospital's decision regarding an evacuation. My mind races with questions. I can hardly walk, I'm so drugged. Will I really have to be unhooked from my IV medicines and port meds? I'm in such a daze. Holding tightly to Rod's hand, he's always here for me. This situation is completely beyond my control. My faith immediately kicks in and I'm praying fervently, despite my drugged state. With Rod at my side, I wait to see how this possible disaster will play out.

Many places in the downtown Pittsburgh area do evacuate, but fortunately for us, West Penn Hospital decides we are safe to stay put. Halleluiah! I don't want my chemo interrupted. How dare an earthquake try to mess up my chemo schedule! Once things in the hospital return to normal, Kathy restarts my meds. This is definitely one chemo session that will not be soon forgotten.

Rod and I celebrate our 32nd wedding anniversary two days later. Because I'm miserable, the only thing we can do together is sit next to each other on the couch holding hands and thanking God that I'm alive. We will celebrate another day when I feel better.

❧ ❧ ❧ ❧ ❧ ❧

Little eyelash and eyebrow hairs are on the bathroom counter as I wash my face. Looking in the mirror, I see what's happening. Are you kidding me? My hair is falling out again! The strong hair around the edge of my hairline that has so valiantly fought to stay a part of me is now coming out in my comb. My eyelashes and eyebrows are falling out, too. This time, instead of tears, I'm pretty peeved.

I ask Dr. Segreti about this, and she tells me that our hair runs in cycles. The fact that I'm experiencing a second round of fall-out is not unusual. Well, I'm pretty angry about it. Now every single strand is going to be gone.

A sore scalp and daily combings of hair loss will not happen again. I root through the bathroom cupboard searching for the electric razor, then call for Rod once it's found. When Rod comes in, I push the razor toward him.

"Here!" I tell him. "Shave it all off! Every bit of it!"

Rod takes the razor from me and says gently, "You will look cute with your head shaved."

I make a face at him.

"*Really*, you *will.*" He doesn't give up. "Your head will definitely look better shaved than with a ring of hair around the edge, and especially better than the bald man 'comb over' hairstyle that you sometimes wear..."

My emotions soften to his voice. "But I *liked* that last ring of hair. It made my hats look cute. Now all of my hats are going to be too big, and I will look like a bald lady who threw a hat on her head."

Rod hugs me and says, "A *cute*, bald lady with a hat on her head. You can just wear your wig more often now."

Rod likes the wig, and so do I. What he says is right. In my dreams, though, I was the lucky person who did not lose her eyelashes, eyebrows, or that last bit of hair. With Rod's reassurance, I decide to be thankful that I hung onto my little bit of hair for as long as I did. We even had our family church picture taken while I still had eyebrows... no eyelashes, but still eyebrows, so why be upset?

Rod begins to shave my head while I stand in the bathtub with a towel wrapped around my shoulders. The last bit of my pre-cancer hair is falling into the bathtub around my feet. Rod continually tells me how much better I look now without those strands of hair hanging like a fringe. He's right, but I still like my hats better with a tiny bit of hair. There are strips of hair you can buy to tape on the inside edge of hats. Maybe I will buy some of those strips.

No tears during this second round of hair loss, just a bit of anger that was quickly squelched.

When Nicolette and Kaycee see me, their young eyes spot something that Rod and I didn't yet notice. Nicolette notices this first.

"Turn around, Mom."

I give her a questioning look. "What for?" Do I really need to give her a model's display of my newly bald head?

"Just do it, please. I want to see something." Nicolette is almost smiling. She wouldn't dare laugh at my shaved head, so something else is making her happy.

"Mom! Your hair is growing back! It's really, really short, but I can see it! Look!" She grabs my arm and pulls me in front of the bathroom mirror. The small hand mirror shows me the back of my head.

"She's right, Mom! I can see it, too!" Kaycee chimes in.

They *are* right! Microscopic tiny hairs are beginning to pop up out of my scalp. It's all white now, but it's beautiful. My hair is definitely growing back! I don't care if it's white! My hair has been color treated since the tenth grade. Dr. Segreti said that blondes' hair often grows back white, and brunettes' hair often grows back gray. No matter, just so it's growing back.

"Thank you, Jesus!" I shout. Losing my hair was one of the most difficult experiences for me. That may sound vain, but it's what made the cancer real to me. When I lost my hair, I could no longer deny its existence.

Just as Lamentations says: *Our God's love does not allow us to be consumed. His compassion is new every morning.*

Earlier today, while Rod shaved my head smooth, I was losing what little hair I had left. That is true, I am. But I'm also growing a whole *new* head of hair. God is good.

∾ ∾ ∾ ∾ ∾ ∾

School has started. I'm restless and want to begin the year with everyone else. Many of my friends remind me that getting well *is* my job right now. There are several teachers covering my position until I'm able to return to work. My goal is to return the second nine weeks of school, which begins November 4. Right now, it's hard to imagine feeling well enough to return to the high energy position of elementary school teacher. Until you perform this job, I'm not sure you can understand the effort truly dedicated teachers put forth. It's a good feeling, though, knowing I help children unlock the key to reading the printed word.

Also, a small part of my job is teaching elementary music classes. It's definitely a full day with little down time, but great rewards. I miss the children terribly. They are like my own.

❧ ❧ ❧ ❧ ❧ ❧

Time for my Day 8 chemo session in Pittsburgh. This is my tenth chemo, only two more to go. The usual five days of feeling miserable after Day 8 come, but exciting days are ahead. We have plans to visit Rod's sister, Leann, and her husband, Steve, in Ohio. They have a three year old son, who brings us lots of laughter. It feels so good to laugh, and I'm ready to be entertained by little Dylan.

Since my surgery in March, I've gone almost nowhere. We're planning a road trip! Let's have a fabulous time.

❧ ❧ ❧ ❧ ❧ ❧

During a quiet time together at home, Rod and I receive a call from Luke wanting to know if we happen to be free one evening. He wants to come over and talk with us. Hmmmm, there is only one topic I can think of that Luke may want to discuss with us when Nicolette is not home…marrying our daughter. We make arrangements for him to visit in a couple of days.

Even though we're concerned about Nicolette getting married when she's just twenty and has her schooling to finish, we're also excited for her. Rod and I spend time in deep discussion sharing how we feel about Luke and Nicolette's relationship, our concerns and our happiness. We know they're young, but so were we. We understand that Nicolette still needs to finish school. So did I when Rod and I married. In fact, I didn't start college until we were married five years and Kaycee was born.

When people questioned the two of us about the logic behind our young marriage, our reply was always that we shared our

Christian faith and believed in the commitment we were making to each other. So do Luke and Nicolette. Thirty-two years later, through thousands of ups and a few downs, we are so happy we married when we did. Of course, we will give our blessing to Luke and Nicolette.

Then Rod laughs and says, "What if Luke is just stopping by to plan a surprise birthday party for Nicolette, or some other small thing, and we've spent all this time planning her engagement?" Fortunately, that's not the case.

When Luke arrives I can tell he's nervous, yet smiling with excitement. He sits down at the table with us. He proceeds to tell us how much he loves our daughter, and that she's everything he hopes to find in his wife. This is a decision that he's prayed about and he's hoping Rod and I will allow him to ask Nicolette to marry him. Luke is so sincere and in love. What a fine young man God brought into my daughter's life.

Rod sits quietly, listening to what Luke and I are saying. He seems to be carefully choosing his words. "I've been praying for a long time about the type of person I would like my daughter to marry. I have this small gift I'm going to share with you to help you understand the type of young man I think will be perfect for her."

Rod pulls out a small object from his pocket and hands it to Luke. When Luke turns the flat, brown object over he discovers that it's a mirror, and he's looking at the type of young man Rod prays for to be Nicolette's husband – himself. This lightens the serious mood, and Luke seems relieved to know that we are extending our blessing to Nicolette and him.

Next, Luke pulls out the beautiful ring he's chosen for Nicolette. It's simple and elegant. Exactly what I believe Nicolette will want to wear. "I looked all over the place to find the perfect ring for her. When I was just about to give up, the saleslady showed me this ring. It sparkles so much that I knew immediately this was the ring for Nicolette. The ring reminds me of her and the way she sparkles when she smiles, she just lights up."

Awwwww, what a guy. He melts my heart, and I thank the Lord that He brought Luke to my precious daughter. It's reassuring to know that if anything happens to me, my daughters have good men to care for them, not just their awesome father, but a husband to stand by them through all of life's challenges.

Our prayer for Nicolette and Luke is from Numbers 6: 24-26 (NIV):

The Lord bless you and keep you; the Lord make His face shine upon you and be gracious to you; The Lord turn His face toward you and give you peace.

God bless them.

∽∽∽∽∽∽

Watching your children become adults are exciting times. It's also a time of transition for parents. On one hand, we wish we could always protect our children, but we have to understand they must make their own way. Through my illness, I've had the chance to witness my daughters growing up before my eyes. At first, I wanted to shield them from the heartaches of this disease, but as we plod through it all, I see that my girls are now young women. They want to be included and be a part of my healing. My view of their place in this health scare of mine has changed over time.

Relationships evolve slowly. It's time to enjoy my daughters beyond my role as mother; it's time for us to be friends, too. We pray our children follow a straight path in God's Word, but also know that we, ourselves, took some side roads at times. We've invested thousands of hours into preparing our children for the world. Now it's time for them to make their own way.

✍ ✍ ✍ ✍ ✍ ✍

Rod and I head out on our road trip. I feel like I'm twenty years old again. Such a long time has passed since we've been anywhere. We first plan to travel to Columbus, Ohio so Rod can inspect a job site. I'll tag along and just hang out where Rod is working. There's always a comfy spot to relax somewhere. Then, we will be off to New Knoxville, Ohio.

When you are in a car together, the opportunity to connect is right there for the taking. We enjoy the ride through Ohio talking and looking back on what has been. Both of us are thrilled that the most difficult part of this journey's end is near.

We pull into Leann's driveway and notice Steve and little Dylan driving around the field on their golf cart. Their Chihuahua, Radar, is sitting on my nephew's lap. They're still at least fifty yards away from us when I put my head out the window to yell "Hello." Immediately, Radar jumps out of the golf cart and runs full speed toward me. I open the car door and he is on my lap snuggling close. He knows I'm not well. The last time this little dog visited us in Pennsylvania, he acted this same way toward me. Prior to being sick, Radar paid me little attention. Dogs seem to have a special sense telling them when a person needs extra love.

Spending time away from home is a welcome respite. We enjoy our visit with our family. They take us with them to watch their oldest son, Rob, play football. It's a chilly night, but what better way to spend a Friday evening in late September. We cuddle up under a blanket with hot chocolate and cheer our nephew on to a victory.

The next day we visit the Fall Festival in Fort Loramie. The weather is gorgeous. Walking around the grounds of the gathering and watching all of the people is entertainment for me. More than entertainment, though, I look more closely at people now. Sometimes you can see that a person is feeling down and perhaps a kind word can change their day.

There are rows of antique tractors at the festival. Dylan is climbing up and onto each one. We're snapping pictures of him looking so cute at the wheel. After we lift him up and down onto every tractor in the row, we spot the sign that reads: Do NOT sit on the tractors! Oops...

Rod decides he has to try some fried Kool-Aid. Have you ever heard of such a thing? This is also the town where Rod fell in love with fried pickles. He's so excited to eat fried food when he gets away from home that he'll try anything fried. I taste his Kool-Aid. It's sweet, but a little too much so for my liking. A super pretzel with cheese is my choice, while the rest of the gang eats hot dogs.

Leann and I find a group of Mennonite girls selling huge pots of fall mums for five dollars each. The open yard is a mosaic of reds, purples, burgundies, blues, pinks and yellows. I want a pickup truck so that we can fill it with dozens of these pots, but I have to settle for two.

These normal everyday activities are like a breath of fresh air to me. Enjoying my family and every moment spent together is more important to me than anything else. These moments remind me that I'm alive! These times help me to keep pushing to the end of this fight. God is good. He guides my every step.

∽∽∽∽∽∽

Time to head back to New Castle and chemo number eleven, a Day 1 treatment. Ugh! I do not want to go back at all. Many times I mention to Rod that my body is done, it really has had enough. I can't take any more of this chemo. He's always the cheerleader who insists I must finish my treatments, especially now that I've come so far.

Nurse Duane is at my door early Tuesday morning, as always, ready to draw my blood. I'm really praying that my counts are good. A celebration is in order because this is my *last* Day 1 chemo coming up. Not that Day 8 is easy, but compared to Day 1, it's not nearly as bad.

Duane always encourages me and keeps his fingers crossed for good readings. Feeling well doesn't mean that my white blood cell counts will be good. I learn that it's a low *red* blood cell count that makes you feel tired. This is the reason I'm always so surprised when my counts are low. Most of the time, I feel really good when they tell me that I'm not able to have chemo.

Later in the day I receive a call from my nurse, Kathy. She's happy about something. The lilt in her voice gives her mood away. I ask, "What's up, Kathy? How are my counts?"

"I am happy to say that your counts are great this week! I will see you Thursday for your session." Kathy pauses for a moment, and then adds, "This is your lucky day, because I have more good news for you."

Now she has my interest piqued. What in the world is she talking about?

"Dr. Segreti looked over your file today, and she decided that this Thursday will be your last session. She said you don't need to come for your last chemo treatment. How does that sound?"

My initial response is that I'm thrilled, but I quickly wonder why it is that I'm able to skip my last chemo. Before I even started my chemo sessions, Rod asked the doctor that if I did really well, was there a chance I would not have to take all twelve sessions. Without a moment's hesitation, Dr. Segreti responded, "No, that's not how it works."

So, why now am I able to skip the last one? Part of me wants to shout, "Halleluiah," but another part of me feels like I'm quitting before I've finished the race.

"Really? Are you sure that's okay, Kathy? I mean, I'll need to ask Rod about that first. He's told me this entire time that I'm not allowed to quit early."

There is a moment of silence. I think Kathy is in shock. I'm sure not many people question when the doctor says they can skip a chemo treatment. "Well, I can check with her again, if you'd like. The last few sessions, though, your body has not bounced back very quickly."

"Yea, I think I have to ask Rod about this. I mean, it's absolutely wonderful if I don't have to go back for Day 8, but I need to see what Rod thinks, okay? Can I get back to you?"

Rod is away today, so I call him with my good news. "Hey, guess what? My white blood cell counts are good to go for chemo on Thursday."

"That's great news." Rod is used to me being delayed the past few sessions due to low counts.

"There's one more thing. Kathy told me that Dr. Segreti said that this can be my last chemo. I don't have to come back for Day 8. As of Thursday, we can be done, if you want."

Rod chuckles. He does not believe me. "You're kidding me, right? Dr. Segreti would *never* let you out of chemo."

"No, I'm serious," I say. "I guess she said my body is telling her that it has had enough. I think that's kind of funny because my body has been telling *me* it's had enough since June."

"Well, what did you say to Kathy?" Rod's voice is elated, not only for me, but for our whole family.

"I told Kathy that I'd have to ask you first."

"What? Why would you say that?" Rod laughs at me. "I'm not a doctor."

"I know, but you kept telling me that I wasn't allowed to quit my chemo early, and that would be quitting early." My mind is programmed to keep going, never dreaming that I would be told that I can do one less chemo.

"*Kimberly*, I didn't mean you can't stop if the *doctor* tells you that you can. I meant I didn't want you to stop because you were giving up. Call Kathy back. Tell her you will be done after this Thursday for sure. Halleluiah!"

Delighted describes it all! How funny that I needed to hear Rod tell me it would be okay to skip my last chemo. We are in this thing so tightly together that it didn't seem right unless I got his approval on that important decision.

Just knowing that I'll be finished with chemo in a couple of days is pure joy. I call my sisters and mother. They are beyond thrilled for me. Treats of banana bread and zucchini bread are baked and arranged on nicely decorated plates, so that I may leave this food gift for the staff at Dr. Segreti's office. They need to know how much our family appreciates all of their care.

Dr. Segreti and Kathy will receive their own special gifts for all the care they have given me. Because of my angel who watched over me during surgery in March, I choose to buy both of them wooden angels as presents. I will give all the special *angels* in my life this same gift at the right time.

✧ ✧ ✧ ✧ ✧ ✧

September 22, 2011, my last day of chemo. Everyone at Dr. Segreti's office is happy for me. They enjoy my banana and blueberry zucchini breads. I must admit they are delicious, but credit for the recipes must be given to my sister, Rhonda. Kathy and Dr. Segreti seem pleased with their angel figurines. A wonderful feeling of peace fills me as I settle into *my chair* for the last round of this awful poison that is making me well. Does that even make sense?

Rod and I are experts at this game now. He sets himself up in his corner office. Kathy gives me whatever she's got that will knock me out; it's easier to sleep through this lengthy process.

Finally, four o'clock arrives, and it's time to head north to New Castle. Hugs and thank yous are shared with Kathy from Rod and me. She's done a lot to encourage me through these past five months since my chemo began. We know we will see each other again soon, but today has a special finality about it.

The trip home is usual. Rod reminds me every fifteen minutes to roll over to my other side to allow the medicine to slosh around in my abdomen. Every awful thing I experience this trip, I just keep reminding myself, *this is the last time I will have to do this.*

When I arrive home, everyone is there to surprise me and celebrate the day. A sheet cake with a special inscription in teal icing proclaims, "Outstanding Job! We love you Kim!" Eleven large teal-colored balloons, one for each chemotherapy treatment, decorate our dining room. We share hugs and tears of joy.

For the next five days I will have IV bags to help with fatigue, and there will be twelve days of feeling miserable, but this is the LAST TIME I am going to feel this way, God willing, in my lifetime.

6

The Slow Climb to Health

Eleven days after my last chemo session my cell phone is ringing at 7:30 a.m. on a Sunday morning.

"Kim," it's my son-in-law, Tim. "Kaycee is at the hospital in labor! Her contractions started at ten o'clock last night, and we came in this morning."

"We will be there as soon as we can!" I'm already shaking Rod to wake him. Before hanging up, there's something I still need to say. "Tim, you and Kaycee are about to witness God's miracle here on earth. Tell Kaycee that she'll forget any pain as soon as she holds our little guy."

Ahhhhhhh! How exciting is this. Trenton's coming to join us. Rod and I lie in bed for a moment longer, talking about how this little baby is going to make our lives change forever. Just the thought of a new generation is exhilarating. Looking at that tiny baby and knowing that a part of him is me, will be one of life's greatest blessings. The cycle of life continues. It's our prayer that Kaycee's delivery goes smoothly. Unfortunately, that's not the case.

Nicolette is thrilled that Kaycee will deliver on a Sunday while she is home from college. Becoming an aunt for the first time will be a highlight in her life thus far. She texts Luke to let him know she is heading to the hospital with us and will not be in church this morning. She wants him to know that he will soon be an *almost* uncle.

We stop at the grocery store on our way into town to pick up some snacks and magazines to help pass the time. The clerk at the store wonders why we're buying so many magazines. Of course, I announce to anyone within earshot, "We are about to become grandparents."

Kaycee endures a long and trying day. The epidural only partially works. After twenty-eight hours of labor a C-section is ordered. Tim is suiting up to go in with her for the delivery.

Dr. Bassaly comes to me. He tenderly cups my cheek in his hand, knowing what I've experienced with my illness this past year. "Do you want to go in, too? Huh?"

My eyes light up. "Yes! Yes, can I? Do you care if I come in with you, too, Kaycee?"

Kaycee waves her hand at me. "Mom, I don't care who is in there with me. I just want Trenton to get here safely. Yes, come in."

On cloud nine, that's me! I pull on the scrubs and light blue booties. Rod ties a mask around my face. Tim and I are ready. Witnessing my grandson being born will be a miracle before my eyes. These moments about to come will be as close to seeing God at work as I may ever witness. All of the frustrations of the past twenty-eight hours will disappear as soon as we meet Trenton.

Nurses begin to scurry around in every direction. Kaycee is disappointed that she is unable to deliver Trenton on her own, but that is what doctors are for, right? They use modern medicine when normal procedures aren't working.

Our family and Tim's family are gathering around the door of the operating room. Tim and I look great in our scrubs. They are prepping Kaycee, and then we will be called in to join her.

We keep watching the door, waiting for our cue to be part of God's miracle. How can anyone doubt that there is a God when you look at the complexities of life? We are so intricately woven together.

When the door opens, it's not a nurse waving us in, it's Dr. Bassaly. He has a look of concern on his face. "The spinal is not working. We will need to put Kaycee under a general anesthetic. The family will not be allowed in the delivery room."

Tim and I are really disappointed, but it's close to 2:00 a.m. on Monday. Kaycee has been in labor since 10:00 p.m. Saturday night. We just want Trenton delivered, as well as Kaycee to be out of pain. This is not the smooth delivery for which I prayed. We are all praying for these past twenty-eight hours to have a happy ending.

The next minutes tick by slowly. It's complete silence in the hallway where we are waiting. We listen intently for any sound of life. I can hear each person breathing, it's that silent. Suddenly, like a halleluiah from heaven, we hear a cry! At 2:03 a.m. on Monday morning, October 3, 2011, Trenton Patrick Aubel announces that he has joined our family. At last, he is here.

Tears flow steadily down my face. We are laughing and hugging each other. What happiness a new baby brings. Trenton represents joy and new life, the future.

How mysterious are God's ways. Never would I dream that Dr. Segreti would say I did not need to complete my twelfth session of chemo. Had I endured one more chemo, I wouldn't be healthy today to be a part of this miracle. Trenton arrived ten days early. If my chemo schedule went as planned, I would be miserable, lying on the couch at home right now. Instead, I'm given this wondrous, glorious day to be with family, celebrating the arrival of our newest member.

Having faced my own mortality makes this day that much sweeter. I'm at peace and say a prayer of thanksgiving for the health of my family.

ꝏ ꝏ ꝏ ꝏ ꝏ ꝏ

At the hospital, while visiting Kaycee and Trenton, I deliver Dr. Bassaly's special angel to him. His early diagnosis saved my life. Not only that, but Dr. Bassaly also delivered both my daughters, Kaycee and Nicolette, and now my grandson, Trenton. Three generations of care have certainly earned him membership in my angel club.

"Dr. Bassaly, I just have to ask you, what was it that made you persist in finding out what was wrong with me? After all of the tests you ran on me with negative results, many doctors would have said, 'Let's wait a year and then see how things are.'"

With a serious expression and his eyes looking upward, Dr. Bassaly hesitates for a minute. "You know, Kim, pictures of my mother and father, who have since passed on, hang on my office wall with a cross between them. They are a big part of the reason I became a doctor of medicine. They believed I have a gift from God for this."

I wait, while Dr. Bassaly appears to ponder his thoughts. "The only reason I can offer you for not giving up is that I feel blessed with a Godly intuition. Yours is not the first case where the tests told me someone's health was okay, but I did not believe it to be true. It is from God when I feel something is not right, and I don't stop until I find out what that is."

I give the doctor a hug. "Thank you for doing your part in saving my life."

"God did this for you, Kim, it was not me." How wonderful to have a doctor who shares my Christian faith.

I start back to work three days a week on Columbus Day. It's a teachers' in-service day, so this lends itself to catching up with friends I've not seen for months. How great to be back among the work force.

A taste of normalcy returns to our home. Working three days a week is perfect. I want to do this all the time. Nicolette is home on the weekends. Her semester at school is going well, in fact, she even made the Dean's list.

ॐ ॐ ॐ ॐ ॐ ॐ

One Sunday evening we drive Nicolette back to college. Rod and I decide to take a walk around the campus. The grass is lush with autumn colors sprinkled across the landscape. We walk at a brisk pace, hand in hand at times. Feeling old is no longer about seeing wrinkles on my face; it's about the state of my health. That saying, *you are only as old as you feel,* has new meaning. Rod and I could pass as college sweethearts, if you could see beyond the surface into our souls.

When we get home, I begin to feel very chilled. I don't have a fever, but I shake uncontrollably. Crawling into bed with a heating pad, I'm still chilled and shaking. Rod crawls in next to me to use his warm body for warmth. He wraps his large arms around me.

"What's wrong with me? Something doesn't feel right. I'm worried. Maybe I'm getting sick again."

"No," Rod assures me. "You are healthy. You might just be fighting a virus or something. Maybe you just over did it. We did take quite a long walk."

"That's probably it." My teeth are chattering. "I took some Tylenol. Hopefully, I'll feel better in the morning."

When I wake up the next day, I feel perfectly fine. It's as if the chills never happened. I get up and dress for work.

Life continues quite routinely for a few weeks. Then, just as suddenly as the first time, I'm overcome by chills. It appears like I'm an addict withdrawing from drugs; this is how much I am shaking. Still no fever, though. We follow the same procedure. First, the bed, then the heating pad, and finally Rod follows, wrapping himself around my shaking body. After about twenty minutes, the chills subside and I feel fine again. In the morning, I push any concerns about my chills aside and get ready for work.

Three weeks have passed since my last chemo session. I need to have a CA 125 blood test before I return for my next appointment with Dr. Segreti. Nurse Duane arrives at New Wilmington

Elementary at 9:00 a.m., punctual as usual. We use a small room in the Nurse's office. It's great that we can do this at school, and I don't need to take off again just for blood work. My goal is to work ten days in October, which I succeed in doing. I offer my highest accolades to the Wilmington Area School District for how they worked with me and supported me all the way back to health.

Time for me to return to West Penn Hospital for scans of my chest, abdomen, and pelvis. They also do a bone density scan. When I see the tall glass of *lemonade* waiting for me, I want to gag already. The nurse is kind and allows me to drink this concoction in the back room, rather than in the waiting room like most people. An observer might get sick just watching me choke the drink down. I can't help it. After all the *lemonades* I have consumed for cleansing purposes over the past eight months, the taste of lemon is now on my nausea list.

When I have three-fourths of the glass in me, I meekly plead, "Is that enough? I'm a really small person. Do I have to drink all of this?"

The nurse chuckles. "That's good. You are tiny."

"Thank you *sooo* much."

The scans do not take long. The dye that runs through me to create a contrast on the pictures makes me feel warm all over. It then proceeds into my body and makes me believe that I have wet myself. At least I know that this time it's just a feeling and not for real.

The next week I have an appointment with Dr. Segreti to review the results from all of my recent tests. I won't lie; I am apprehensive. If any of my scans come back with bad reports, I'll be surprised. But I can't shake the memory of the day Dr. Bassaly was concerned about my health, and I dismissed his worries as being overly cautious, only to learn I had cancer. Please let that not be the case today.

Dr. Segreti opens the door with a serious face. "First, your scans and CA 125 tests are great. There is no sign of cancer at this point in time." Rod and I smile at each other. "You do have osteopenia, but for now, all we want you to do is take calcium and Vitamin D tablets."

I exercise daily and use light weights already, what more can I do? Taking the calcium and vitamin D sounds easy enough. Hopefully, this will be enough to stop the osteopenia from progressing into osteoporosis. Dr. Segreti says that they will continue to monitor this condition.

Dr. Segreti continues. "I don't like the sound of these chills you're having. Tell me about them. Are you running a fever?"

"No, no fever, just uncontrollable chills. Rod has to hold me just to keep me somewhat still. They're pretty bad, but after about twenty minutes, they're gone. It's only happened twice." I am curious why she's concerned.

In her matter-of-fact, no-nonsense style, Dr. Segreti says, "We are going to have Kathy pull your PICC line today. When you have a line inserted for this long, there's always a chance that bacteria can grow on the line. We want to get that line out of you."

Wow, I didn't expect this on my visit today. It never dawned on me that the PICC line could be causing my chills. "Will that hurt?"

The doctor shakes her head. "Nope, Kathy will numb it up, and slip it right out. I'm going to put you on an antibiotic, just in case we discover bacteria on your line."

Hooray! Another event to check off of my list! My PICC line has been my friend these past five months. No needle pricks when I had chemo, blood drawn or dye scans done. But – I can't wait to get this thing out of my body! We are parting ways. Tonight, for the first time in five months, I can shower without Rod plastic wrapping my arm. Standing any direction in the shower stall is acceptable now, and best of all, no flushing out the PICC line tonight. We can begin to take all of the chemo supplies out of my dining room and put my home back in order.

Dr. Segreti is right. It takes Kathy only a moment to numb my arm and pull the PICC line. She wraps the PICC line up and sends it off to the lab to be tested for bacterial growth. At home, there are still quite a lot of the heparin and saline syringes used to flush my PICC line left. Kathy tells me a West Penn Hospital doctor is going on a trip to the Philippines soon. I'm pleased that I'm able to donate all of my extra gauze pads, alcohol swabs, and syringes.

Despite the excellent care that Rod and Nurse Duane gave me, do you know that PICC line actually *did* have bacteria? I'm amazed, because there's nothing we could have done to take better care of the line. After my day at the hospital – no more chills. Problem solved. Next on the list, get the port out!

The following Friday I'm scheduled to have the port removed from my abdomen. When this day arrives, we're not surprised at our long wait. Dr. Segreti is in major surgery again. We wait in the short stay department from late morning until closing time. They move me from short stay to recovery, because short stay is shutting down for the day. Then, it's time for all the nurses in recovery to go home. One stays, just for me.

Finally, Dr. Segreti is free for me. It only takes about fifteen minutes to remove my port. When I wake up, I'm the only patient in the recovery room. I place my hand on my abdomen. Other than a few stitches and numerous battle wound scars, I have a normal stomach again. My body is back. No more foreign objects inside. My head rests back on my pillow, and I whisper, "Thank you, Jesus." I'm smiling in my bed for no one at all. Only God can see me. I'm sure He knows my smile is for Him.

Soon Rod is by my side. "We're almost at the finish line, kiddo." He brings my hand to his lips. "You did good."

"No," I say. "*We* did good." We pray together, thanking God for providing us with the strength and sustenance to reach this point.

ᗡᗡ ᗡᗡ ᗡᗡ ᗡᗡ ᗡᗡ ᗡᗡ

With many medical milestones behind me, it is time to begin looking forward. Nicolette is excited to start planning her wedding, and I'm certainly happy to focus my attention on all of the preparation activities. Finding her dress is the first thing on our list.

At some point in time, every mother thinks about the tender moments of shopping with her daughter for her wedding gown. Nicolette, Kaycee, Trenton, and I undertake this adventure one brisk October morning. I didn't anticipate this being a difficult decision. Each dress Nicolette tries on looks stunning on her. She has a striking figure, and she's a beautiful girl. (Can you tell I'm her mother?) Typically, she is not a picky shopper. I envision us finding her dress at the first shop we visit. Wrong.

Each gown that Nicolette tries on is just *okay*. Nothing is giving her that *Say yes to the dress!* feeling. I know what she is talking about. When I shop, I pretty much know what the look is I want, but finding that look in a dress is not always easy. Kaycee and I are very patient at the first four stores, but we begin to wear thin. Trenton is a real trooper at just one month old. Nicolette just keeps saying, "I'll know it when I see it." I begin to wonder if the dress has even been created yet.

Finally, we tell Nicolette that this is the last stop of the day. She agrees. The moment we step into the fourth boutique, Nicolette spots a dress on the sale rack. "That's it! I love this dress!"

Kaycee looks over the gown. "You're right, Nicolette. I love this, too. Try it on."

I'm thanking the Lord above. These two children never agree on styles of clothing. They are like night and day, the moon and the sun, need I go on? But on this wedding dress, they both agree.

When Nicolette walks out in the chosen gown, my tears flow—tears of joy. How do I explain this moment in words? It is like a vision from a pleasant dream. My oldest daughter, a brand new mother, stands before me holding her perfectly beautiful son, my first grandchild, while my youngest daughter wears a pearl white lace-covered gown, looking like an angel from above. Months of cancer treatment are finally finished, and I appear to be in great health now. It is a precious moment. A perfect moment in an imperfect world that I will never forget.

∽∽∽∽∽∽

Now that chemo is behind me, it's time to get back to taking care of the rest of me. I get my eyes checked and my teeth cleaned. A visit to the podiatrist is scheduled for him to check my two toes that give me pain when I walk. My knee joints are hurting. In fact, for a couple of weeks I wonder if I may have a fibromyalgia of some sort. Every nerve and muscle in my body seems to be hurting.

The neuropathy in my hands and feet is not improving, it's getting worse. In fact, if I need to get up in the night, I shuffle as if I'm eighty years old. In the mornings, it takes a good fifteen minutes before I fully feel my feet. Luckily, once the blood is flowing, the feeling in my feet improves substantially. Once I get to work, I'm able to maneuver around as if all is well.

One morning, I wake up and feel as if someone has slammed my fingers in a door. There are rings across my nails. As the days pass, I notice that my fingernails begin to lift off of my fingers. I keep trimming them as short as possible to try and prevent catching one on something, causing it to break off completely. There is an underlying layer of what appears to be jagged skin, or nail that didn't form. This layer is extremely soft and difficult to trim, but it's awful looking, sticking out from underneath my nails.

As a licensed manicurist and having worked as a nail technician for five years, I never saw anything like my own nails on any of my clients in my salon—except for a woman going through cancer. As much as I dislike how my nails appear, this is all quite interesting to me.

Talking with my friends who have gone through this, we all seem to have different experiences with our nails after chemo. One friend tells me her nails turned black, so I decide to be positive about this, do not complain, and just keep my nails painted all of the time. At least I do not have black nails. No one notices the problem I'm having with my nails, as long as they are painted. Fortunately, I only lose one nail at the mid-section.

ᘐ ᘐ ᘐ ᘐ ᘐ ᘐ

One morning I notice a bulge from my stomach right at the top edge of my scar. When I ask Nurse Duane about it, he tells me to cough as he places his fingers upon the bulge.

He almost smiles and shakes his head, almost in disbelief. "I think you've got a hernia."

"You're kidding, right?" I can't believe this. The last thing I need right now is a hernia.

"Does that mean I'll have to have another surgery?"

Nurse Duane is smiling now. "No... I mean you could, but a lot of people live with these. I'm not even sure this is one, but you need to show this to Dr. Segreti when you go back to Pittsburgh."

I call Dr. Segreti's office about some of these problems. The nurse practitioner tells me that the neuropathy can take up to a year to go away. There's a chance it may not go away completely. As far as my joint pain, Dr. Segreti says that chemo does not typically affect the joints. Her thought is that the steroids I was taking masked the strain I placed on my knees when exercising. Now that the steroids are leaving my system, I'm aware of the inflammation in my knees. As far as the hernia, Dr. Segreti will look at that at my next appointment. If it's not bothering me, it will be fine.

Hmmm, always something. I'm weary of all the side effects resulting from my chemo. They are nothing different than what many people experience all the time. In the grand scheme of life, these are minor health annoyances.

∽∽∽∽∽∽

Thanksgiving arrives. For our family, this is truly a year to offer thanks to God. Our year is really turning around – all good things. Rod's family has their Lutz family reunion on Thanksgiving Day. My mother-in-law comes from a family of nine children. Our church's gymnasium is used for the celebration since there are over one hundred relatives arriving. So much news to catch up on. The day has become bittersweet. For each new member added to the family, there seems to be another member we lose. I'm extremely blessed to still be with this group of wonderful people for another year. Everyone showers their blessings on me and extends their love and prayers.

∽∽∽∽∽∽

Once a year, my sisters and I travel together to Pittsburgh for our annual mammograms. Mom started us on this tradition, but now that she's in Florida she misses out on this trip. We girls laugh to the point of tears, to the point of stomach aches, several times during the day. We laugh at each other and at nothing at all. Years are added to our lives on this day just from laughter.

It's surprising to me that Dr. Segreti says I must keep my mammogram appointment this year. With all of the scans I had for her, I thought my mammo was covered. She tells me I must be very diligent about any type of cancer screening, since I'm now in a higher risk group from already having had cancer.

I wouldn't want to miss my colonoscopies or mammograms, would I? They're such fun, right? Of course they are not fun, but they save lives. I am diligent about following doctors' orders. I'm tested out the wahzoo and probably glow in the dark.

Normally, I get my mammo just because my mother and doctor say I should. This year, I feel differently. I pray all is well and say my 1,000th prayer of thanksgiving since my illness began. My mammo is clear.

This mammo trip is a great opportunity to present both Rhonda and Jamie with angels for all of the time and support they generously gave, and continue to give me.

∽∽ ∽∽ ∽∽ ∽∽ ∽∽ ∽∽

Christmas is fast approaching. Another angel is packed up for my mother and sent off to Florida. My daughters and Ali also receive their very own angels to mark this year as one filled with blessings and healing. I want to give Rod an angel, but he says a new kitchen sink is good enough for him. We visit the home improvement store and pick out a new sink.

The holiday season offers a much needed break from school. I probably started back to work fulltime a little sooner than my body wanted. The extra rest will be good for me.

Rod and I can't wait for New Year's Eve. We are planning something that we've not been able to do since I became ill. We pass up a couple of invitations to spend this evening with friends and family. Nicolette is curious why we want to stay at home rather than coming out and celebrating with others. Ahh, the innocence of youth. Nothing will keep Rod and me from celebrating tonight, but tonight, we just want to be alone. We have an entire year upon which to reflect. This New Year's Eve will be one of our best yet.

The weather is chilly, but not too cold. Rod and I put on our bathing suits and wrap up tightly in soft, fuzzy towels. We head outside, kicking off our flip-flops, dropping our towels, and on the count of... 1... 2... 3... we sink down into the Jacuzzi together. "Ahhhhh..." Life is good.

The water is bubbling warmly around our necks. I laugh, almost giddy, savoring the feel of the jets massaging my back. We lay back our heads and look up at the stars. God knows I only enjoy the hot tub on clear nights and it is gorgeous outside. What a year 2011 has been. We toast each other with our pretend champagne, kiss the New Year in and rejoice for today. We don't know what tomorrow brings, but today is blissful, and I finally get to go in the hot tub again. Here's to 2012!

∽ ∽ ∽ ∽ ∽ ∽

In January, it is already time to have new scans and blood work done. This is a big day because not only am I having my scans again, but Nicolette is scheduled for a bone marrow biopsy with a doctor at West Penn. It's been almost a year since she was first ill.

Her white blood cell count is still very low. The doctor wants to make sure we're not missing something.

Our plan is for me to go upstairs and have my scans done, while Rod goes with Nicolette. Whoever finishes first will meet up with the other later. I walk into the nurse's office just off the waiting room for x-rays. There it is, my *lemonade* waiting for me again. Ugh!

"Please don't make me drink all of that. Three quarters, maybe?" I take off my coat. "I'm really small, remember me?"

The nurse shakes her head and gives me a knowing look. "Do the best you can."

I gag it down. My size trick seems to work again. I think I'll use it every time they hand me one of these drinks.

Within an hour I'm done at X-ray, so I head down to Nicolette's doctor's office. Grabbing a magazine, I settle into a comfy chair to read. Being back to work, I don't have much time anymore to just relax. How does that happen so quickly? I went from a life where the minutes ticked away one at a time, so slowly I wanted to cry, to a time so busy I don't know how to get everything done in a day.

Fifteen minutes pass, then a nurse comes out looking for me. She sits close and puts her arm around my shoulders. Immediately, I am thinking, *what is wrong? Has something gone wrong with Nicolette's procedure? Please God, let everything be okay with her.*

These thoughts are racing through my head, when the nurse smiles. "Now I don't want you to worry. Nicolette is fine... it's your husband."

"What?" This is the last thing I expected to hear from this nurse. "What's wrong? Is he okay?"

She pats my arm. "Your husband is fine. The poor thing passed out on the floor when your daughter started groaning a little. The doctor was trying to take out a tiny sample of bone, and this caused Nicolette some discomfort. Your husband is about as white as the walls. We have him lying down in a different room."

Awwww, I feel so bad. I rush to Rod's side, while Nicolette finishes her test on her own. Rod feels a little embarrassed, but I don't know why. I did not even want to go in with Nicolette, so I can understand why her pain made him feel lightheaded.

He is resting on the floor of an examining room when I step in. "Hey, Big Guy, what happened?" Smiling for him, I crouch down.

My knight in shining armor, this stoic man who has witnessed with valor all of the dreadful scenes that cancer causes, is now weakened to the floor by his daughter's pain... even Superman has his kryptonite!

"I'm fine." Rod grabs my hand. "I knew I was going down. I kept saying, 'I need a place to sit down,' but no one was paying attention to me. They were focused on Nicolette, and then finally, I started heading toward the floor. The nurses got me this far, and then I went down. I'm okay, though."

"It's all right now." I run my fingers through his hair and soothe him.

When the doctor peeks in to see how Rod is doing, my husband pipes up, "Hey, Doc, I guess being your assistant is out of the question, huh?" That's when I know he is doing fine.

Everyone laughs. Rod is upset because he was really interested in what the doctor was doing. He felt okay watching until Nicolette seemed to be in pain. The doctor assures him that he did quite well, and that if it was the doctor's daughter having the test done, he doubts that he could watch the test, either. We seem to have such excitement any time we visit West Penn Hospital.

The good news is that Nicolette's tests are clear, and she simply has a low white blood cell count. She also has allergies that affect her health, but it is nothing too serious. In the past year, we discovered that Nicolette has a thyroid problem and is anemic. All treatable conditions, we are relieved and thank God for his goodness.

More fun activities are starting. My niece, Dana, is getting married, so we have her shower and wedding fast approaching. All of these celebrations make life extra fun. Both Kaycee and Tim's birthdays are soon, and Lisa is going to have a baby girl in late March. We will be honoring her at a shower this month, too. How amazing that life is getting back to normal. How many times did I ask myself last year if life would *ever* be normal again? My prayers are answered.

 භ භ භ භ භ භ

I just woke up, and already there is a joy deep down in my soul. It is March 1, 2012. I am a one year survivor. It's hard for me to wrap my head around this past year and all that has transpired. Do you remember that old childhood Sunday school song, *"I've got the love of Jesus, love of Jesus, down in my heart. Where? Down in my heart. Where? Down in my heart. I've got the love of Jesus, love of Jesus, down in my heart. Where? Down in my heart to stay."* Let's shout that song to the rooftops.

The joy I'm feeling is far beyond the surface. It's bubbling up from somewhere down deep in my soul. If I could, I would whirl and twirl up and down the hallways at school today.

When I arrive at work, I share this wonderful news with some of my friends. My friend, Kathy, tells me an eerie story of this time last year. One day I was at school working with her side by side, and then she didn't see me again for the rest of the school year. All she remembers is that I left my snow boots beside my desk that last day, and those boots sat there next to my desk every day from then on, but I never came back. My name tag hung by my door, but I was not the person sitting at my desk. She tells me how thrilled she is about my one year survivorship, and that she is glad those boots are no longer in my room.

Ali, always the creative one, has designed a *follow the teal-colored road* around the hallways of the school. Today I feel like Dorothy in *The Wizard of Oz*. While walking students to their classroom from my Title I Reading room, I notice the first sign. It says: "Happy One Year Anniversary." Hmmm, something seems fishy. Then, I spot the second sign: "You are an inspiration!" Ha, ha! I'm onto this. At the time, I don't know it's Ali who is responsible for this unique way of honoring my special day, but I'm not surprised when I discover it is her.

As I walk the halls of the school, these signs are everywhere. Some say "Determination," some say, "We are so proud of you!" Thank you, Jesus, for bringing me to this place in my life. It is good.

My special friends are included in today's celebration. They have their own survivor stories to celebrate. I put a sign at Marjorie's desk: "1 Year Survivor!" I put a sign at Anita's work station: "6 Year Survivor!" I put a sign at Linda's desk: "10 Year Survivor!" And I proudly stand next to the sign Ali has posted by *my* door: "1 Year Survivor!"

At 3:45 p.m. I call Ali to my room where we snap a picture next to my sign. It is one year ago to the minute when I was prepping for our Family Math Night and I listened to the message from Dr. Bassaly's receptionist asking me to come to his office. Ali and I stand exactly in that same spot where last year I received that ominous phone call. This year we hug in celebration of a year gone by, but never forgotten.

✧ ✧ ✧ ✧ ✧ ✧

Today Trenton arrives at seven twenty in the morning. Poor little guy has viral pneumonia at five months old. I start by rubbing some Vicks into his chest. Then I try to feed him a bottle, but he's only interested in about two ounces. I'm wondering if he is fussy because his throat hurts, or perhaps it is his chest. He fusses back and forth over the next hour with the bottle until all four ounces are finally in him.

At lunch time, Rod and I drive to the medical supply store to buy the nebulizer ordered by the doctor for him. It's so cute. It is a nebulizer in the shape of a yellow car. When Trenton is older, I know he will think this is cool. I give him some Tylenol. Then, I hold him squirming around on my lap while Rod holds the misty end of the nebulizer to his nose. This is definitely a two person job.

After his breathing treatment, he actually takes a one and a half hour nap. His sleep is not sound, though, because if I so much as try to put him down, he's upset. He cries, and he cries hard. He lets you know that you need to be attending to him. I sit and hold him for an hour and a half. I treasure every minute.

Thankfully, as the day progresses, both Rod and I believe that Trenton is making a turnabout. When Kaycee arrives to pick him up she laughs. "What is the matter with both of you?"

Rod is standing there with a heating pad wrapped around one knee with an ace bandage holding it in place. The wire to the heating pad is hanging from his leg, so that when he returns to his office he can just sit down at his desk and plug it in! I have a brace wrapped around my back and waist to give me added support while carrying Trenton.

We look at each other and shake our heads. "I think your parents got old overnight," I say.

We smile. Getting older means I am still alive and have a purpose. Watching Trenton today was not easy, but I enjoyed every moment. When I hold him up on my shoulder, and his little hands cling to me, depending on me to take care of him during his illness, being his Nana is one of the greatest gifts God has bestowed upon me during my lifetime. Rod and I pray daily that Trenton grows to be a Godly man.

⚭ ⚭ ⚭ ⚭ ⚭ ⚭

My list of things I need to get through in order to finish this journey is fast approaching its end. Being a person that needs a sense of at least moderate control, I created a list to check off events as each milestone is complete. Another day of milestones is here. Tonight I'm getting my hair colored. I may finally be able to go out minus my wig. Right now I have a full head of short, kinky, curly white hair.

My beautician, Becky, will need to wave her magic wand over me. Turning this *Brillo pad* into something stylish will definitely need an *abracadabra* or two. My tab this evening will be expensive, but everyone says Becky's the best around. After years of frugalness in regards to my hair, Rod says that it's time for me to splurge on myself.

I ask Becky if she is willing to see me when the salon is closed rather than going into a crowded salon and whipping off my wig. Awkward—vanity is a vice. God bless her, she will see me at 8:15 p.m. I arrive right on time as her last client is leaving.

Becky sits down next to me. "So, tell me what direction you want to go, Kim. Do you want your roots darker and highlights put in, or are we just putting one shade in to get started? Tell me what you're thinking."

I have to laugh. "It doesn't matter what you do to my hair tonight, anything will be better than this." The white fro on my head makes me look like a Q-tip! "Work your magic, if you can."

She stands up, adjusts her apron, and heads to the chemical room. "Okay, let's do it. I'm up for the challenge."

I like this girl. She has spirit and is determined that I will leave her salon feeling better about myself. We compare our life missions as we converse through the evening. I share with her that God has placed me in the classroom to touch children's lives in a meaningful way. Each morning on the way to school I recite the fruits of the spirit, asking God for... *love, joy, peace, patience, kindness, goodness, faithfulness, gentleness and self-control* (Galatians 5:22 NIV). May I portray these fruits to every child with whom

I come in contact with each day. My students need to feel better about themselves when they leave my classroom.

Becky feels the same. She says that her mission is to help everyone leave her salon with more confidence and a higher sense of self-esteem. This gives her a great feeling, knowing that she helps people feel significant. I'm glad to hear this, because confidence and self-esteem are what I need right now. Don't get me wrong, I'm not complaining. I'm so thankful just to have hair again, even if it's white and really curly and short.

The fun begins. Becky explains that since it has only been six months since my last chemo, residual chemicals remain in my system. These will interfere with the coloring process. When I select my desired shade of hair, that doesn't mean I will get that shade. My body's chemical makeup is out of balance and this will affect my hair coloring. It will be like a science experiment. She's going to have to do a lot of mixing to arrive at an acceptable hair shade.

I pick up on the code language Becky and her assistant, Linda, use as they work with my hair. First, Becky tries a brown shade on my hair. Linda rinses the color and the two of them exchange a, *"That's better than it was,"* with each other. When I stand under the light, Becky says "Oh, my, it looks like mud... muddy brown. This will never do. Let me try this."

I think to myself, *better than it was,* means not good.

She goes back into her chemical closet and pulls a few more tricks out of her bag.

Here, Kim, let's add a touch of this." She squirts a different shade onto my hair. Linda rinses it. "That's *better,*" Becky says.

"Yes, it's better," Linda agrees.

When I stand under the light, Becky says, "Oooh, I don't think so... too violet." Back to the chair to try something else.

I think to myself, *better,* means okay, but still not good.

Becky must try about five different shades before I finally hear, "That's *much* better."

"Yes, *much* better," Linda agrees.

I think to myself, *much better,* means it's time to go home!

"Okay, if it's *much better* now, not just *better,* let's stop here," I say.

As I look at myself in the mirror, my thoughts travel back to the day when I last sat in this exact spot. On that day, I was losing my hair and Becky was fitting me for my wig. It was one of the first times I cried about my cancer.

But now, my eyes well up with happy tears. "We've come a long way in the past year, haven't we? I remember sitting right here almost a year ago while you were styling my wig for me."

Becky looks surprised. "You're right! Oh, my, we have come a long way since then." Then more quietly she almost whispers, "I'm just glad you are still here to sit in that chair!"

Me, too, I think... me, too.

When I arrive home, Rod thinks my new hair style is wonderful. "It makes you look younger and sexy. I feel like I have my young bride back," he says. His mother certainly trained that boy right, didn't she?

❀ ❀ ❀ ❀ ❀ ❀

Six hours later, the alarm is ringing and it's time to pray for courage. What is everyone at school going to think about my hair?

Ironically, I was scared to wear a wig in public for the first time, but now, when it's time to go *without my wig*, I'm afraid of that, too.

At first, I feel overwhelmed and think about just throwing the wig on top of my head. Rod convinces me to at least try and style my hair, and if I have no success by a certain time, *then* put the wig on.

I fuss with this and that, use the flat iron and burn my ear. My hair is still so short. Finally, just as I'm ready to give up and don my wig, Rod offers to help me. With hair product all through my hair, Rod starts pulling hair every which way, giving me a spiked do. Guess what? I love it! The children will probably not like my hair, simply because children don't like change, but they will get used to my hair soon.

Praying for a positive attitude and a sense of humor, I head off to school. To tell the truth, I'm so happy to be wigless, I don't think it will matter what anyone says to me today.

When I arrive at school, I am the *hot topic* of the day. The first words out of the kindergartners to their teacher are, "The music teacher cut off her hair!"

Today, my sense of humor is my greatest strength. As I enter a classroom, one second grade boy yells, "You look like a boy with earrings!" Really? Come on! Is it that bad? No, these words do not take me down. I love my hair, my very own hair.

A little second grade girl lets this boy have it, "She does *not*, she looks like a rock star!" I love that girl. "You know what, Mrs. McCormick? If you put a stripe of pink down your hair, you'll look like my favorite singer, Pink! I love your hair! It's great!"

This comment lifts me up and makes me feel a little better. That is until some of the first graders see me. One of my dear students looks at me and asks, "What happened to you? You're scary!"

Really? Scary? I thought this was a sweet, little boy. He just called me scary. I smile and say, "It's short and sassy, not scary." Those are great words – short and sassy, yes, I like that.

The funniest compliment I receive all day is from a first grade boy. He runs up to me and says, "Mrs. McCormick, do you know who you look like? You look like the Snow Queen from that play we saw this year, do you remember her?"

"Why, yes I do. I think I like looking like a queen. That's pretty cool."

"There's just one thing you need to do to *really* look like her." This boy is so excited about me looking like the queen character. He jumps up and down, wanting so badly to blurt out his thoughts.

"What do I need to do to *really* look like the Snow Queen?" I'm very interested in hearing this answer.

He is smiling from ear to ear. "You just need to turn your hair *white!*"

Laughter bursts forth from me with little control. If this sweet little boy only knew how much money I just spent to get *rid* of my white hair. Guess what? No Snow Queen for me.

∽ ∽ ∽ ∽ ∽ ∽

Today, I'm packing away the old. I'm a new person now, a changed person. I can never go back to who I was, because life's experiences change us, and I've certainly been through a life-changing experience.

Since my illness, I'm more keenly aware of the needs of people around me. I always tried to be caring toward others, but now I'm more willing to give up my free time to make a difference in someone else's day. Surviving cancer makes me a better person; at least I'm always *trying* to become a better person. Life was always precious, but is even more so now.

All of my senses are more profoundly acute. When I breathe in the soft, pleasant scent of Trenton with his tiny face up against mine, I soak his baby scent in, lingering there, remembering every second. Looking at God's world around me, I spot the tiniest insect working with its crew, building up its home, and I'm amazed at God's handiwork. When my family laughs together, there's no more chuckling, it's just good ole' belly laughs, rejoicing at the thrill of life and love. And when those muscular arms of Rod's wrap themselves around me, I will always remember this time in our lives, and how our strong love grew even stronger. Every day is now lived with passion.

As I pack away my hats, my wig, and the head huggers that go under my wig, I look fondly at each one as it is placed inside the box. These items have served their purpose well. They are special to me. They were worn to many different events, giving me some style. I wore my khaki hat with the leopard spotted buckle to school one day when my hair was just beginning to fall out. The students told me I looked like I was going on a safari. I *feel* like I have been on a safari and was chased by lions and tigers and wild boars.

My blue pageboy hat will always be a favorite. I wore it to my last chemo session. Now, *that* is a special hat!

My white pageboy hat with navy sashes that wrap over my ears and tie behind my head went on many walks with Rod and me. It was privy to all of the serious talks we shared on those walks, it heard me cry many times, and rejoice when we were able to walk at our pre-cancer pace.

There are several others that I pack away, along with memories of some days happily forgotten. Other memories made and lessons learned while wearing the hats, I will cling to for a lifetime.

Even though the hats are cute, to wear them now would transport me back to a time that I choose to leave behind me. I consider donating them, but realize there is always the chance that I will have a recurrence and will need this box again. The box is tucked into my bedroom closet. We pray that it stays there forever. I don't want to have any reason to share these items with any family member, or to use them myself, ever again.

ഇ ഇ ഇ ഇ ഇ ഇ

It is time for Easter break. Other than Christmas, this is my favorite holiday. Knowing that Christ died for us to save us from our sins, then rose again to live with our Holy God, is reason to celebrate. It is no coincidence to me that Easter is during the spring. This is a time for rebirth and hope.

The day of our 4th grade Music Program is finally here. You can tell something is up at our school today, as the children are dressed so beautifully. The boys' and girls' excitement is contagious. Hours and hours of hard work have been put into this program, today they get to experience the fun of performing.

We hold a dress rehearsal for the school for students in grades K-3, as well as for any parents who choose to attend the daytime performance rather than the evening performance. The energy in the air is almost visible. We have students dressed up in 1960s garb to sing and dance to music from *Hairspray*. There are students acting out roles from *Spiderman*, while the choir sings Michael Buble's version of the theme song. A group of girls are dressed in soccer outfits and will perform a dance to "Waka, Waka," the theme song from the 2010 World Cup Soccer competition. They have soccer balls and dance while doing passes and tosses with the balls. Students are playing recorders, bongo drums, and maracas. Others will dance the limbo. Do you see what I mean? Activity abounds.

The students' afternoon performance is incredible. The little ones in the audience cheer for Spiderman as he rescues a damsel in distress from a bandit. The crowd claps along with our rendition of John Denver's "Grandma's Feather Bed." When it's time for the final song, "How You Live," by Cindy Morgan, I pray for strength. The lyrics from this song have become part of my family's inspiration for the past year. I want this year's music program to have a profound effect on those attending. My prayer is that everyone leaves our show with a renewed sense of hope and purpose in their life.

During our rehearsals, my friend is so moved by the lyrics to "How You Live," that she asks how I feel about sharing the lyrics with the crowd. What a fantastic idea. The words are included in our show's program. When I introduce the song, I ask each person to think about the words they hear while we sing. Perhaps they may wish to hang the lyrics on the refrigerator, or somewhere that the words can be read frequently. The lyrics remind us how precious life is, and just how precious each child is. When I'm done introducing the song, I'm crying. Even though I promised myself I would not, I can't help it.

The students sing this song with their hearts. Children are singing so hard that their eyes are squinting. I love these kids. When the song is finished, members of our audience are also crying. Our music has touched their hearts. I feel as if I just directed a choir of small angels. This is my mission, to touch the hearts of these children and their families for God. Of course, I can't come right out and say that in a public school setting, but I ask that God's light is shining through me today.

I pray the music we sing fills the children's spirits with joy and hope. It may be only a small seed planted in my students, but another day, many years from now, someone else may experience the joy of seeing that seed bloom.

੭ ੭ ੭ ੭ ੭ ੭

Time for another three month appointment with Dr. Segreti in Pittsburgh. My blood work is taken and sent to West Penn Hospital. I look forward to seeing all of the girls there. It's as if the nurses go through your illness with you. Walking down the hall toward Dr. Segreti's office, I see Karen, one of the nurses. She lights up and yells, "Kim! How are you?"

I give her a hug. "I'm doing great!" I fluff her hair. "You changed your hair. I like the darker shade!"

"Yea, it's a little darker now." Now it's her turn to fluff my head. "And you changed your hair, too." She smiles.

I know what she is thinking without her saying anything more. "Yes... you don't even have to ask. This is my own hair. It feels great to have hair again."

In the waiting room, I see Bernie, another one of my nurses. She gives me another big hug. Bernie weighs and measures me, and then we go into an examination room. As soon as the door is shut behind us, her eyebrows raise, and she smiles wide, lifting her hand for a high five. This is a good sign. Now I know that my tests are all clear! This will be a wonderful day.

Typical new grandmother that I am, Trenton's Easter picture with the live bunnies and chicks sitting next to him is shown to everyone. The staff here is aware that I postponed a chemo session for this little guy's baby shower. They want to see who it is that is so important to me. I have never seen a baby who is not cute, but they give the appropriate oohs and aahs to make me feel that my grandson is extra special.

Bernie looks at her watch. "We're running a little behind. It's so busy in here today."

"That's not a good thing." I frown. "That means a lot of other people have cancer." This is a disturbing thought for me.

Bernie shrugs her shoulders. "But, the doctor is here for the people who need her. That's what's important."

I agree, but I can never stop thinking about the need for a cure. Surely, in this day and age, someone will discover a cure for cancer... *all* types of cancers. People have conquered other diseases of epidemic size, why is it that cancer outsmarts us?

I remind myself that we *are* conquering cancer. Every day we get closer to a cure. Perhaps even ten years ago, I may not have survived this disease. Progress is being made, just not fast enough.

Dr. Segreti and her nurse practitioner enter the room. I am examined. All is well.

When Dr. Segreti is leaving, I ask her one final question. "I know you cannot give me an absolute for an answer, Dr. Segreti, but in your best educated opinion, how do you think I got cancer? Someone like me, who does nearly everything right, eats right, exercises regularly... what do you think?"

With just a few seconds of think time, Dr. Segreti looks at me. "Endometriosis. Medical research is finding that there seems to be a link."

Hmmm, this gives me a degree of explanation since I suffered with endometriosis in my teens and twenties, but it also gives me an uneasy feeling. Kaycee had a severe case of endometriosis recently, and I'm concerned as to what this may mean for her in the future. Medical research has to prevail. God has given great wisdom to mankind. In the meantime, I commit myself once again to doing my part in giving back.

Rod and I pray together in the evening, thanking God for another victorious appointment in Pittsburgh today. When we hold hands in fervent prayer, our love for each other strengthens. We know we are blessed. Along with blessings comes the responsibility of doing for others. Once we understand life is not about us, but about serving others, it becomes that much more meaningful.

ॐ ॐ ॐ ॐ ॐ ॐ

Our days fill with planning a wedding shower for Nicolette and Luke. The family unites, once again, in preparation. Rod cooks up egg casseroles and French toast with a maple syrup. Hope and Luke's sister, Kelly, add a variation on these dishes. There is a huge fruit bowl with pineapple, strawberries, red and green grapes and blackberries. Best of all are the orange glazed cinnamon rolls— Pillsbury blue ribbon winners.

With family and friends helping, we look like an assembly line in an upscale New York kitchen, everyone with their special job, Rod filling the role as head chef. He loves this. We agree that he missed his calling. Perhaps in retirement, he can start a catering business. Although, that might take all the fun out of it.

Kaycee has all of the decorations under control. The shower is themed on vintage couture with lace, ribbon, and candles decorating the church gym. Lovely. Amazing. A gymnasium is transformed into a setting of celebration. That girl has talent she does not even realize she has.

Guests arrive and distribute items for Nicolette's cupboards on a round table. They were asked to bring goods beginning with the first letter of their last names. Kleenex, Ziploc baggies, rosemary, toilet paper and much more are donated to the cause. It's a table of fun to help Nicolette fill her first pantry as a married woman.

Luke arrives with Nicolette's favorite flowers in hand, yellow lilies. We play the typical question and answer game where the guests witness how well the bride knows her future groom. For every wrong answer Nicolette gives, the bridesmaids flash an embarrassing picture of Nicolette from her youth on the wall, pictures from her days of wire-rimmed glasses and braces.

Nicolette does so well answering the questions, that I give Kaycee permission to project *all* of the pictures anyway. It's in good fun, and the pictures aren't really embarrassing, just extremely cute and funny.

Showering Nicolette and Luke with gifts is certainly what our family and friends do. I am truly blessed by all the people in my life.

The evening is spent at Dave and Buster's in Pittsburgh. Wedding party members, our family and the O'Haras (Luke's family) enjoy supper together. Entertainment in the game room follows. Most of my time there is spent pushing Trenton around in his stroller. He is fascinated by the screeches, toots, and blinking lights of the arcade.

When we finally call it a day and arrive back home, Rod and I fall in complete exhaustion into bed.

"When did we get so old?" I cuddle into a pillow and curl up ready to sleep.

"We're not old," Rod says. "We haven't stopped for the past forty-eight hours. Anyone would be tired."

I smile contentedly. This is how life is meant to be lived, the special ordinary every day moments that make up family life. *Pray without ceasing.* I thank God for the 2,000th time since becoming sick for allowing me the pleasure of being so tired, emotionally spent, yet delighted all in the same moment. Life is good.

ぬぬぬぬぬぬ

Mother's Day, 2012. Today is an extra special Mother's Day. Trenton is being dedicated in the early church service at First Baptist Church. At the church, family members sit in the front pews. We get preferential seating, so that we may see this joyous occasion up close and personal.

The children and babies are escorted onto the stage by their parents. Trenton is the first baby introduced. The Children's Director shares with all of us how Trenton is very pleasant and outgoing. Right now, his eyes are round like saucers, as he displays his wonder at the mass of staring people. He must be thinking, *Why are all of these faces smiling at me?* He is mesmerized.

Lines of commitment are recited as we promise to assist in bringing these children up in a Christian belief system. Every day Rod and I pray for Trenton's life, today and in the future. His little life is a miracle, as is my own. We ask that he be wise beyond his years as he grows, making good decisions and living his life in honor of our Lord Jesus Christ. As the saying goes, "It takes a village to raise a child." I look down the two rows filled with our family members here in support of Trenton, Kaycee and Tim. We certainly have the village!

I sometimes ask myself what significant events are yet to unfold in my life, events in which I will play an important role. Events that will help me understand why God saved me from cancer. Trenton's life is one of these. One day he will understand that his life helped to prolong mine.

❧ ❧ ❧ ❧ ❧ ❧

Rod and I walk in the sunshine that so brightly lights the after-noon sky today. It has been months since I basked in sunlight. Chemo makes your skin sun sensitive. Sitting only ten minutes in the sun last summer resulted in huge, red blotches all over my skin. I was destined to sit in the shade all summer and fall. It's a new spring this year. Closing my eyes, I spread my arms out wide, lift my head to the heavens and smile. Let the sun shine on me, and let God's Son shine through me! I am a new person, and I am healthy!

It is not possible for me to survive this disease and not give back in some meaningful way. For this is part of my obligation, part of my religious heritage and part of the reason I live. Writing and teaching are two ways in which I can tell my story and hope-fully assist others in early detection and treatment. Just knowing my story and how I survived and what sustained me may be of help to others and make their journey somewhat easier. And per-haps I can raise some funds for research.

❧ ❧ ❧ ❧ ❧ ❧

It is *Relay for Life* week in my hometown, New Castle, PA. How rewarding for me to realize that a group of fourth graders orga-nized a fund raising event at my school. They call it *Crazy for a Cure*. Each day the staff and students are to wear special outfits in honor of the fight against cancer. In order to dress *crazy* each day, we must donate to the cause. Monday is *Crazy Sock* day. Tuesday is *Crazy Shoe* day. Wednesday is *Crazy Hat* day. Thursday is *Pink*

Out day, and Friday is *All out for a Cure* day—combine them all. There are balloons and student-made posters all around the school. When *Crazy Hat* day rolls around, I'm surprised that I am able to go to my special hat box and take one out to wear. When I packed these away, I vowed to never open this box again unless a loved one or I was in need of the hats. My spiritual healing is moving forward. I feel okay about wearing one of my hats so soon again. Wearing one of my cancer hats is a great way to promote fighting for a cure. My JLo hat is a favorite among the students, so I plop it on. How wonderful it feels to wear my hat with a full head of hair underneath it! Let's get this *Crazy* party started.

The students raise nearly six hundred dollars for the American Cancer Society. They give me a *Kickin' Cancer* t-shirt. I'm honored and touched by their compassion. We can win this battle. With the next generation already fighting alongside of us, how can we lose?

⋘ ⋘ ⋘ ⋘ ⋘ ⋘

> *Those who hope in the Lord will renew their strength.*
> *They will soar on wings like eagles; they will run and not*
> *grow weary, they will walk and not be faint.*
> Isaiah 40:31

The day is picture perfect, a clear blue sky and a high of eighty degrees. If I was able to order the ideal day for the *Relay for Life Walk*, this is it. Between the excitement of the event and the celebration of this final milestone, my stomach is a bundle of nerves. On our way to the event, Kaycee calls my phone. "Hey, Mom!

Do your best! We're thinking of you! You know we'd be there with you, if we could! We love you!" I'm thrilled with her call. Tim and Kaycee have an appointment in Pittsburgh today and are unable to attend the *Relay for Life Walk*, but her hugs come through the phone line.

We arrive at the high school early to register for the walk. White tents surround the field, people are milling about and purple shirts are everywhere. Purple is the color of survivors; along with my teal, it's another great color for blondes. The quote on the back side of our survivor shirts says: *Life is not about waiting for the storm to pass; it is about dancing in the rain.* I would love to dance in the rain with Rod.

A Walk-A-Thon is one of the day's features. Participants are sponsored by others who promise to pay a certain sum for each lap walked. Money pledged for this purpose is donated to cancer patients in need and cancer research.

The announcer calls all of the survivors and their caregivers to the starting point on the track. The opening ceremonies begin with a Survivor/Caregiver Walk. This also happens to be National Armed Services Day, and there is a troop of National Guardsmen standing at attention as we prepare to walk. The members of all the relay teams, as well as family and friends, are asked to line the inside edge of the football field. The ribbon is cut and the sea of purple begins moving forward.

We feel like movie stars on the red carpet walk. People are cheering and clapping for all of us, letting us know that they're proud of us for what we've been through. Music is blaring out of the large speakers, probably heard a mile away. The atmosphere is electric. Applause from the crowd does not stop during our entire walk around the field. If I could, I would take off running.

During the entire walk I'm thankful that Rod is included, too. He was by my side through this whole ordeal. It's fitting that we take this walk to the finish line hand in hand. Flashbacks of the past year and a half rush forward to the present. Days of pain, healing, nausea, IVs, trips to Pittsburgh, chemo, hair loss, sleepless nights, endless hours of fatigue... they're all over. Tears trickle down my cheeks, as I squeeze Rod's hand tightly during the entire walk. This is far more emotional than I anticipated.

Several yards before the end, I see my family and friends waiting for us. Nicolette and Mom are close to the edge. I run to give Mom a hug, then grab Nicolette, pulling her along to join us as we near the end of this road. We are victorious soldiers returning home from battle. God is our leader. He does not promise us that life will be free of sorrow and difficult trials, but He does promise us He will always be there to guide us through... wrapped in His arms of love.

We arrive at the end of the walk. We are finished. This battle is over.

Post Script

Dear Readers,

While fighting the deadly disease of cancer, I had hours of time in which to study the scriptures. These are just a few of my favorite verses. They provide me with strength, encouragement and joy. May the Lord bless you with His words. May they provide you with peace and comfort in your own trials, as well as uplifting you during life's celebrations.

In God's love,
Kim

♥

Kim's Favorite Scripture Verses

In times of worry:

Philippians 4:6-7 (NLW)
> Don't worry about anything, instead pray about every-
> thing... tell God what you need and thank Him for all
> He has done... if you do this you will experience God's
> peace which is far more wonderful than the human mind
> can understand... His peace will guard your hearts and
> minds as you live in Christ Jesus.

Matthew 6:34 (NIV)
> Therefore do not worry about tomorrow, for tomorrow
> will worry about itself. Each day has enough trouble of
> its own.

Matthew 6:26-27(NIV)

> *Look at the birds of the air; they do not sow or reap or*
> *store away in barns, and yet your heavenly Father feeds*
> *them. Are you not much more valuable than they? Who*
> *of you by worrying can add a single hour to his life?*

I Peter 5:7(NIV)

> *Cast all your anxiety on him because he cares for you.*

Psalm 55:22(NIV)

> *Cast your cares on the Lord and He will sustain you; He*
> *will never let the righteous fall.*

In times of fear:

Joshua 1:9 (NIV)

> *Be strong and courageous. Do not be terrified; do not*
> *be discouraged, for the Lord your God will be with you*
> *wherever you go.*

Philippians 4:13

> *I can do everything through Him who gives me strength.*

Hebrews 13: 5-6

> *...Never will I leave you; never will I forsake you.' So*
> *we say with confidence, The Lord is my helper; I will not*
> *be afraid...*

Isaiah 41:10 (NIV)

> *So do not fear, for I am with you; do not be dismayed,*
> *for I am your God. I will strengthen you and help you; I*
> *will uphold you with my righteous right hand.*

Psalm 46:1(NIV)

> *God is our refuge and strength, an ever-present help in*
> *trouble. Therefore we will not fear...*

In times of discouragement and sorrow:

Psalm 34:18(NIV)

> *The Lord is close to the brokenhearted and saves those*
> *who are crushed in spirit.*

Lamentations 3:22-23(NIV)

> *Because of the Lord's great love we are not consumed, for*
> *his compassions never fail. They are new every morning;*
> *great is your faithfulness.*

II Corinthians 1:3-4(NIV)

> *Praise be to the God and Father of our Lord Jesus Christ,*
> *the Father of compassion and the God of all comfort, who*
> *comforts us in all our troubles, so that we can comfort*
> *those in any trouble with the comfort we ourselves have*
> *received from God.*

Psalm 3:3(NIV)

> *You are a shield around me, O Lord; you bestow glory on me and lift up my head.*

Psalm 23:1-3 (NIV)

> *The Lord is my Shepherd, I shall not be in want. He makes me lie down in green pastures, He leads me beside quiet waters, He restores my soul.*

In times of rejoicing:

Romans 5:3-5(NIV)

> *...we also rejoice in our sufferings, because we know that suffering produces perseverance; perseverance, character; and character, hope. And hope does not disappoint us, because God has poured out his love into our hearts by the Holy Spirit, whom he has given us.*

Jeremiah 29:11 (NIV)

> *For I know the plans I have for you, declares the Lord, plans to prosper you and not to harm you, plans to give you hope and a future.*

Psalm 150:6 (NIV)

> *Let everything that has breath praise the Lord.*

Isaiah 49:13 (NIV)

Shout for joy, O heavens; rejoice, O earth; burst into song, O mountains! For the Lord comforts his people and will have compassion on his afflicted ones.

Isaiah 40:31(NIV)

Those who hope in the Lord will renew their strength. They will soar on wings like eagles; they will run and not grow weary, they will walk and not be faint.

The song, "How You Live," became an inspiration to my family and friends during my time of illness. It is my prayer that the lyrics to this song, sung by Point of Grace and written by Cindy Morgan, will be an inspiration to your family and friends as well.

How You Live

Wake up to the sunlight with your windows open,
Don't hold in your anger or leave things unspoken.
Wear your red dress, use your good dishes, make a big mess
and make lots of wishes.
And have what you want but want what you have.
And don't spend your life looking back.
Chorus: Turn up the music, turn it up loud.
Take a few chances, let it all out.
'Cause you won't regret it,
looking back from where you have been.
'Cause it's not who you knew, and it's not what you did,
It's how you live.
So go to the ball games and go to the ballet.
And go see your folks more than just on the holidays.
Kiss all your children, dance with your wife.

Tell your husband you love him every night.
Don't run from the truth, 'cause you can't get away.
Just face it and you'll be okay.
(Chorus again.)
Wherever you are and wherever you've been,
now is the time to begin.
So give to the needy and pray for the grieving
Even when you don't think that you can.
'Cause all that you do is bound to come back to you.
So think of your fellow man.
And make peace with God and make peace with yourself.
'Cause in the end there's nobody else.
(Chorus again.)
'Cause it's not who you knew and it's not what you did,
It's how you live.

For more information on ovarian cancer go to
www.foundationsforwomenscancer.org or www.ovarian.org

You can contact Kim regarding speaking engagements or
questions about *Wrapped in His Arms of Love* via email at
wrappedinhisarmsoflove@gmail.com

Like us on Facebook at
www.facebook.com/wrappedinhisarmsoflove

**All profits from book sales will be donated to the Pittsburgh
Chapter of the National Ovarian Cancer Coalition (NOCC),
and the American Cancer Society.**

WA